Critical Lawyering Skills

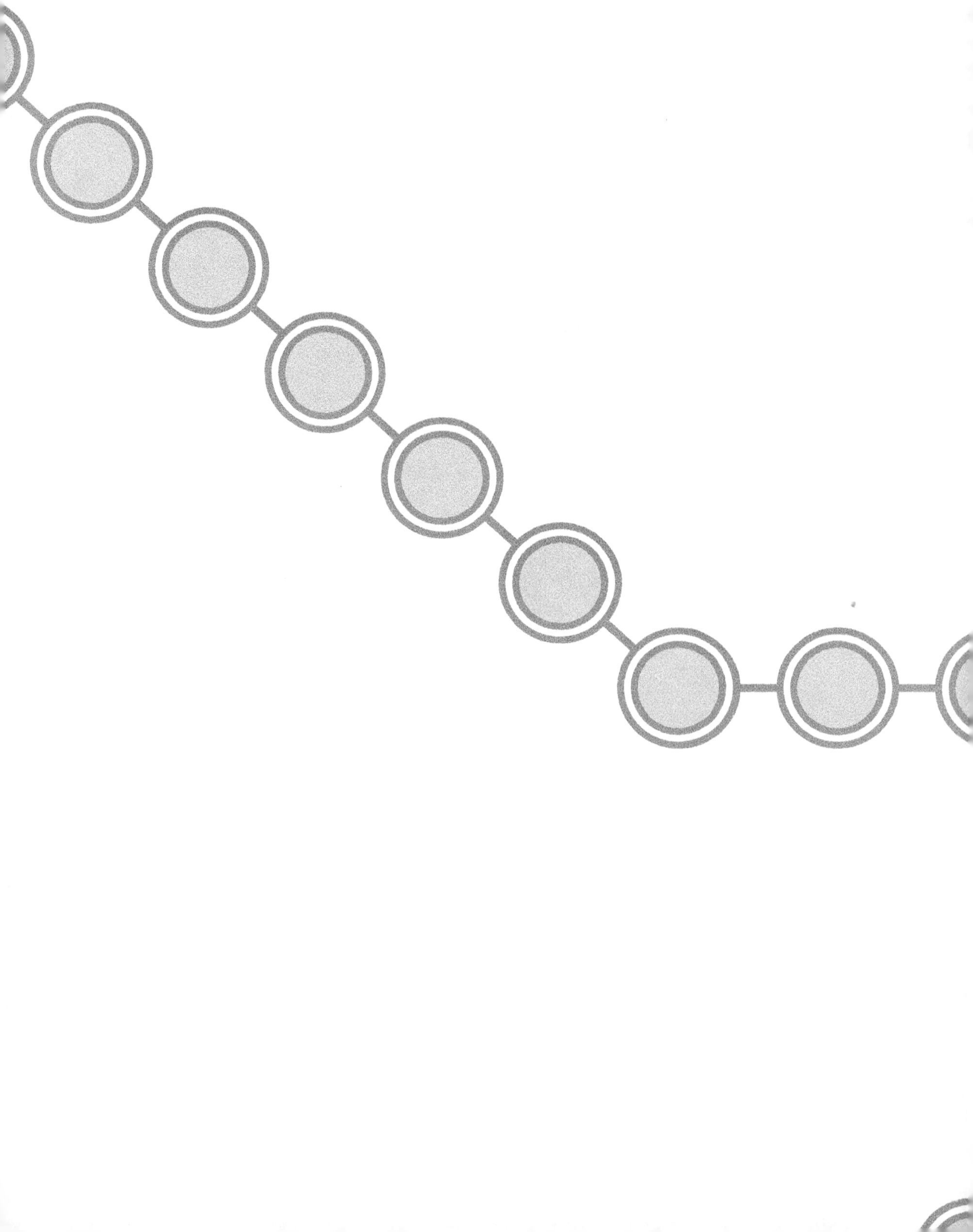

Critical Lawyering Skills

A Path to Professional Identity

Thiadora Pina

CAROLINA ACADEMIC PRESS
Durham, North Carolina

Library of Congress Cataloging-in-Publication Data

Names: Pina, Thiadora, author.
Title: Critical lawyering skills : a path to professional identity / Thiadora Pina.
Description: Durham, North Carolina : Carolina Academic Press, 2025. | Includes bibliographical references and index.
Identifiers: LCCN 2025001611 | ISBN 9781531032111 (paperback) | ISBN 9781531032128 (ebook)
Subjects: LCSH: Practice of law—United States. | Law—Study and teaching—United States. | Lawyers—United States. | Legal ethics—United States. | Law—Vocational guidances—United States.
Classification: LCC KF300 .P55 2025 | DDC 340.023/73—dc23/eng/20250116
LC record available at https://lccn.loc.gov/2025001611

Carolina Academic Press
700 Kent Street
Durham, North Carolina 27701
(919) 489-7486
www.cap-press.com

Printed in the United States of America

Contents

Critical Lawyering Skills

1 Critical Skills and Professional Identity

LEARNING OUTCOMES

- Recognize that lawyers often work in teams and partnerships.
- Explain and illustrate the importance of relying on solid, objective evidence in communicating professional identity and development.
- Name the top ten skills critical to a lawyer's professional identity.

Critical Lawyering Skills:
The Path to Professional Identity Formation

Welcome to Critical Lawyering Skills (CLS).

This workbook is designed for law students who plan to practice law after graduation. As you transition from law student to lawyer, you will develop your professional identity. Critical Lawyering Skills helps you build that identity intentionally, rather than leaving it to chance.

Developing a strong professional identity is crucial for success in the legal field. The best—and most fulfilled—professionals understand their interests, skills, values and goals, and align them with their actions as a lawyer. The CLS workbook provides practical tools and exercises to help you navigate this process effectively.

By using Critical Lawyering Skills, you will be better equipped to make informed decisions about your professional path and to develop a professional identity that supports your values and aspirations. Additionally, it guides you in appreciating and internalizing the ethical obligations that lawyers have to their clients and society. By engaging with the CLS material, you will gain a clearer perspective on your role as a lawyer and the responsibilities that come with it, which will serve you well as you transition from law student to practicing attorney.

What Is Professional Identity?

According to the American Bar Association's Section of Legal Education and Admissions to the Bar, "[p]rofessional identity focuses on what it means to be a lawyer and the special obligations lawyers have to their clients and society."[1]

Many law students think they have a good idea of "what it means to be a lawyer," or, at the very least, they think they will figure it out on their path to becoming one. And what about the "special obligations lawyers have to their clients and society?" Perhaps that sentence gives some students pause, but, once again, many students think they will figure that out too as they travel along that same path.

The path that we are talking about, or the path that students think they know or will figure out, is the path to professional identity formation. But there is a better alternative to the "I'll figure it out along the way" approach. Several studies have al-

1. ABA Standards and Rules of Procedure for Approval of Law Schools 2023–2024, https://www.americanbar.org/content/dam/aba/administrative/legal_education_and_admissions_to_the_bar/standards/2023-2024/23-24-standards-ch3.pdf.

ready defined the path. It turns out that the path to a lawyer's professional identity formation includes mastering several competencies or critical skills.[2]

Students will study the critical skills new lawyers must develop and demonstrate in order to successfully enter and thrive in the profession. The workbook format of this book will help you develop these skills by practicing them.

The skills required to build a student's professional identity are unique to the field of law. Thus, even if you already have post-graduate employment or other substantial work experience, you likely have not developed the critical lawyering skills necessary for the practice of law. You will not learn about or practice many of these skills in the general law school curriculum, not even in your elective classes. And, neither will you learn these skills working for non-legal employers.

Your Path from Student to Lawyer

This class will help you to identify, develop, and ultimately demonstrate and communicate these skills to future legal employers and clients. Walking the path of professional identity requires you to internalize these necessary critical lawyering skills so that who you are personifies "what it means to be a lawyer and the special obligations lawyers have to their clients and society."

How will students do this? You will start by remembering and defining the critical lawyering skills identified in this text that will help you to develop your professional identity. You will then apply this information as you practice becoming an expert in self-reflection and self-assessment—two skills that are crucial in building your self-development as a lawyer. You will also map your learning to existing rubrics, like the one shown in the table on the next page.

As you develop stronger skills, you will measure your progress and set goals for yourself so that, as your professional identity develops, you will be better prepared to gain employment during law school, be a successful new lawyer, achieve meaningful employment and appreciate your obligations to your clients and society.

Here is a visual representation of the professional identity formation path that you will climb.[3] It begins with identifying the necessary critical lawyering skills, and it ends with your authored professional development plan.

---

2. It is noted that the terms "competency" and "skill" may have distinct meanings depending on context: competencies often refer to a combination of skills, knowledge, and behaviors, and skills often refer to individual abilities. However, these terms will be used interchangeably throughout the workbook.

3. The Northeast Texas Consortium of Colleges and Universities, *Bloom's Taxonomy*, https://www.netnet.org/for-faculty/course-development/blooms-taxonomy/ (last visited Feb. 22, 2021).

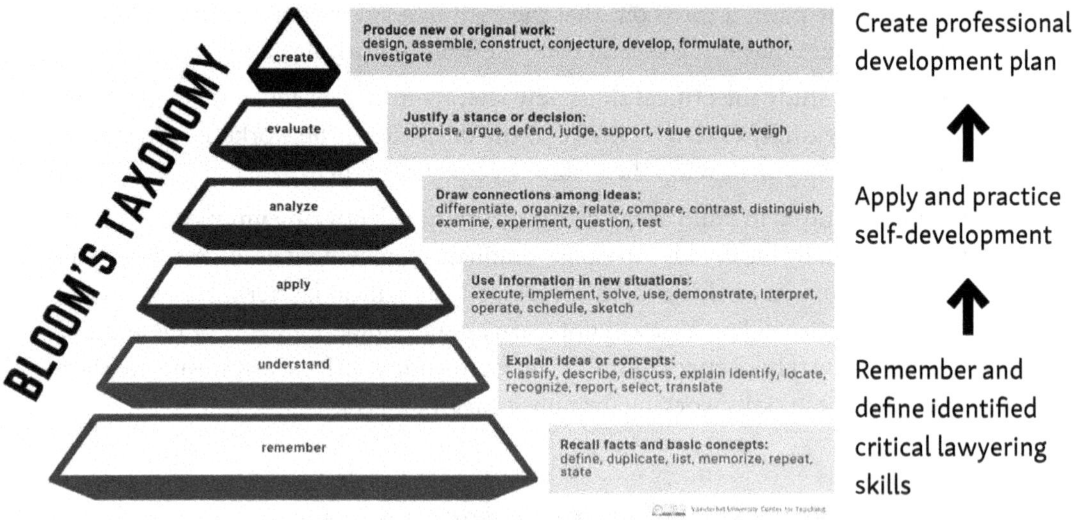

Using Rubrics

Because rubrics provide multiple benefits, this workbook relies heavily on several of them. Rubrics provide clear criteria for performance, promote objectivity, offer structured and focused feedback, encourage reflective thinking, and ensure consistent evaluation. Because they offer objective, solid evidence, rubrics are particularly helpful when it comes to helping you build your professional identity—something you will see more clearly as you work through the assignments and rubrics found in the next several chapters.

Importantly, rubrics also help to combat what is known as the Dunning-Kruger effect,[4] an effect that is certainly relevant to law students. For our purposes, the Dunning-Kruger effect is a cognitive bias where individuals with lower knowledge or expertise in a particular area overestimate their competence, while those with high competence may underestimate their relative skill. This phenomenon suggests that the less someone knows about a subject, the less aware they are of their lack of knowledge.

Because you are in the earliest stages of your legal career, the Dunning-Kruger effect is particularly relevant. Rubrics will thus provide the clear and objective criteria needed to accurately measure and assess your skills. The first rubric you will use appears immediately below, and you will use this rubric to complete your first assignment (more on that in a minute).

4. D. Dunning & J. Kruger, *Unskilled and Unaware of It: How Difficulties in Recognizing One's Own Incompetence Lead to Inflated Self-Assessments*, 77 J. PERSONALITY & SOC. PSYCHOL. 1121–34 (1999), https://doi.org/10.1037/0022-3514.77.6.1121.

Rubric: Law School Professional Development Initiatives in the First Year[5]

Sub-competencies of lawyering skills	Commits to excellence and high-quality work (work that meets expectations and demonstrates complete effort)	Seeks and Incorporates feedback
Novice (Level 1)	Often submits less than high-quality work.	Rarely seeks feedback.
Advanced Beginner (Level 2)	Occasionally submits less than high-quality work.	Occasionally seeks feedback and makes improvements based on the feedback.
Intermediate (Level 3)	Almost always submits high-quality work.	Regularly seeks feedback and makes improvements based on the feedback. Begins to proactively develop mentor relationships to receive feedback.
Student at Graduation (Level 4)	Always submits high-quality work.	Creates and uses a cyclical feedback loop to evaluate the effectiveness of activities and makes improvements. Proactively develops mentor relationships to receive feedback and often meets with mentors.
Junior Attorney (Level 5)	Always submits high-quality work and regularly delivers beyond assigned tasks to exceed expectations.	Meets Student at Graduation criteria and, in addition, meets with existing mentors in regular intervals to receive feedback.

CLS Workbook Organization

This is likely the first time you have used a workbook in law school.

The path to professional identity includes mastering several critical skills, but these skills must be practiced and not simply studied. Thus, a workbook format is best suited to building your professional identity because you will practice and demonstrate the skills you learn. Also, because "[r]esearch indicates that informa-

5. Adapted from the Holloran Center for Ethical Leadership, *Professionalism: Honoring Commitments Milestone*, University of St. Thomas, https://law.stthomas.edu/about/centers-institutes/holloran-center/competency-milestones/honoring-commitments-professionalism/index.html (competency milestones database) (last visited Dec. 2, 2024).

tion recorded by hand is more durable in the memory than information recorded by machine,"[6] you will handwrite most of the exercises and homework that are due.

Each chapter begins with specific learning objectives so that you will begin with the end in mind. In other words, you will begin each chapter knowing what you should be able to do by the end of that chapter. Each chapter also has a learning assessment and reflection section: remember, becoming an expert in self-reflection and self-assessment are two crucial skills to building your self-development (and professional identity) as a lawyer.

Your Continuous Resource

Your professional identity includes internalizing and practicing the critical skills necessary to move from being a student to being a successfully practicing lawyer. To do this, you must develop and improve over time, acting differently—or better—at the end of this course (and the end of law school) than you did at the beginning.[7] You will thus take the processes you learn and practice in this class and apply them to your remaining time in law school and beyond.

This workbook is intended to be a continuous resource for you to refer to, add to, and refine as you continue on your professional identity path. You are starting your legal career; knowing the necessary critical skills and the path to professional identity will help you better navigate the road ahead.

Let's get started!

Pre-Class Work

> *"The road for successful entry-level lawyers and meaningful employment requires... a much broader blend of legal skills, professional competencies, and characteristics that comprise the whole lawyer."*[8]

---

6. Pam A. Mueller & Daniel M. Oppenheimer, *The Pen Is Mightier than the Keyboard: Advantages of Longhand Over Laptop Note Taking,* 25 PSYCHOL. SCI. 1159, 1166 (2014) (finding students who took notes on laptops performed worse when asked conceptual questions on material).

7. R. Lisle Baker, *Designing a Positive Psychology Course for Lawyers*, 51 SUFFOLK U. L. REV. 207, 249 (2018), https://ssrn.com/abstract=3271713. Thiadora Pina is indebted to R. Lisle Baker for providing this paper.

8. Alli Gerkman & Logan Cornett, *Foundations for Practice: The Whole Lawyer and the Character Quotient*, at 5 (2016), http://iaals.du.edu/sites/default/files/reports/foundations_for_practice_whole_lawyer_character_quotient.pdf.

1. Identify and Communicate Your "Elevator Pitch"

You may be familiar with the term "elevator pitch." An elevator pitch is a brief and persuasive pitch that can effectively communicate who you are, what you do, the professional value you bring, and your objectives.

Ideally, this pitch highlights your background, current experiences, and future aspirations while making a clear connection to the person or organization with whom you are speaking. As a law student, the clear connection you will make here is to your goal of securing legal employment, which may be securing your first legal internship or externship, for example; if you know what type of law you want to practice, your objectives may be more precise. But either way, you always need an elevator pitch.

Draft your elevator pitch in the space provided here.

____

____

____

____

____

____

2. Update Your Résumé and Bring a Copy to Class 1

The education section of your résumé must include, at a minimum, your current law school information.

You will need to reference your updated résumé to complete the Pre-Class Work below.

Bring a copy of your updated résumé to class 1. You will use it during the Chapter 1 In-Class Activity. You may use either a hard or soft copy.

3. What Is Solid Evidence in Regard to Professional Identity?

Review the *Law School Professional Development Initiatives in the First Year* rubric above.

This rubric identifies two skills which law students are expected to master in their first year of law school: *commits to excellence and high-quality work*, and *seeks and incorporates feedback*. Thus, at this stage of your legal career, you too should be able to demonstrate these two skills.

Demonstrating a skill requires more than simply stating that you have that skill, however. Demonstrating a skill requires solid evidence. You must show your skill level by providing an example of "a time" when you developed and relied on that skill. Your résumé is one way to accomplish this.

As you know, your résumé is used to present a summary of your qualifications, including your education, work experience, skills, and accomplishments. Its primary purpose is to provide potential employers with a quick and clear overview of your professional background and to demonstrate why you are a suitable candidate for a job.

It is essentially a marketing document that sells your professional capabilities to potential employers. And, at this point in your career, your professional capabilities should clearly demonstrate, at a minimum, that you commit to excellence and high-quality work and that you seek and incorporate feedback (as a way to improve your performance).

4. Exercise: Demonstrating Critical Skills with Solid Evidence

Instructions:

- Focusing on your résumé, choose a job description you have listed which clearly demonstrates the two skills identified above in the *Law School Professional Development Initiatives in the First Year* rubric.
- Next, select your current development level from the first column, and use the table below to list the *solid evidence* you are relying on to demonstrate that you are at the stage you selected.
- You must be able to pull the solid evidence you are relying upon directly from your résumé. If you cannot, perhaps you need to update your résumé?

Lawyering Skills	Development Level	List *solid evidence* for your selection
Commits to excellence and high-quality work (work that meets expectations and demonstrates complete effort)		
Seeks and incorporates feedback		

Pre-Class Work Complete

In-Class Activity

1. Class Discussion: Introductions: Strong Team Relationships and Effective Oral Communication

Welcome to our first in-class activity. You will note that each CLS chapter begins with class learning objectives. These objectives will drive all Pre-Class Work and In-Class Activities, and each activity will help introduce the critical skills you will develop on your professional identity formation path.

This first activity will focus on the following two skills:

- Initiates and maintains strong team and work relationships.
- Effective oral communication.

We will soon go into greater detail about how these two competencies fit within our class learning objectives, but for now, let it suffice to say that the following activity focuses on these two competencies.

This activity also recognizes, often contrary to how many law school classes are structured, that "partnerships have long been the preferred form of professional organization for lawyers"[9] and that lawyers often work in and with teams.

Instructions:

- Partner with a classmate whom you do not know and introduce each other to the class. Your presentation will include three things the two of you have in common that are not obvious to your classmates.[10] You and your partner will decide who presents which of the three commonalities.
- You have five minutes to complete this activity.

Commonalities	
1	
2	
3	

9. *See* Baker, *supra* note 7, at 207.
10. *Id.*

2. Class Discussion: Your Elevator Pitch

- How did you choose your strongest skills?
- How did you determine employer value?

Note: You will revisit this assignment in Chapter 7 when you are asked to compare and contrast your Chapter 1 and chapter 7 Elevator Pitch assignments.

3. Activity: Relying on Solid Evidence from Your Résumé

Instructions:

- ▹ With your partner from the In-Class Activity, review your entries from the Demonstrating Critical Skills with Solid Evidence exercise in the Pre-Class Work section above.
- ▹ Answer the questions below, paying particular attention to the efficacy of the "solid evidence" your partner relied upon for the sub-competencies of the *Law School Professional Development Initiatives in the First Year* rubric.

- Is the evidence my partner provided solid? Why or why not?

- Does my partner's résumé adequately support their chosen "solid evidence"? Why or why not?

4. Class Discussion: What It Means to Be a Lawyer

Which skills, characteristics, and traits do new lawyers need to have internalized and be able to clearly demonstrate immediately upon entering practice? They are the same skills, characteristics, and traits that help form your professional identity and that legal employers and clients need, want, and value. This is why it is important that you take the time to develop and practice these critical skills as a law student.

Fortunately, several studies have already identified these critical skills. We do not have to guess or rely on individual ideas or experiences to understand how law students can begin to develop their professional identity and how they can best prepare to enter the legal market and thrive as practicing lawyers. The work has been done for us.

The following five studies are key to identifying these critical lawyering skills:

Foundations for Practice (IAALS) (2016)

Attorneys General/Non-Profit (ROADMAP) (2018)

Small and Large Firms (ROADMAP) (2018)

Predicting Lawyer Effectiveness (Shultz/Zedeck) (2011)

Building a Better Bar (IAALS) (2020)

Collectively, these studies surveyed over twenty-four thousand lawyers in all fifty states. These lawyers represented many practice areas, such as corporate law and criminal law. They also represented many practice settings, including in-house attorneys, solo practitioners, attorneys who work in non-profit organizations, and large and small law firms.

a. The Special Obligations Lawyers Have to Their Clients and Society

Working in the field of law means that you will serve clients. Your client may be an indigent person in an underserved community, a corporation, or a judge. There are endless possibilities in terms of who your client(s) may be; however, regardless of the type of law you practice, you will have a client.

Being aware of your client's needs is a key component of your success in building your professional identity and transitioning from law student to lawyer. It is important to know that building your professional identity will also support retaining, serving, and providing excellent customer service to clients.

Throughout this book, you will focus on and practice how to better understand and work with legal clients. You will also focus on the special obligations lawyers have to society. You must always remember that lawyers are the stewards of the legal system in the United States. And, in the United States, one of the chief ways we try to mete out justice is through the legal system. It is not only the criminal law system that works this way—our legal system itself is centered on this principle.

5. Class Discussion: Which Critical Skills?

Which skills did the five studies referenced above identity as critical? Let's find out!

Instructions:

- Below is a general list of lawyering skills. However, when the data from the surveys identified above are reviewed in the aggregate, ten of these skills bubble to the top of the list.
- Circle the ten skills you think the lawyers who answered those surveys chose as being critical to developing professional identity. As you make each selection, have a reason for that choice in mind. Why do you think that skill is critical?

List of Lawyering Skills

Negotiation skills	Stress/crisis management	Leadership
Delegation, supervision, mentoring	Initiative/drive/ strong work ethic	Commitment to and pursuit of professional development and self-directed learning
Good judgment/ problem solving, including appropriately engaging supervisor	Integrity/honesty/ trustworthiness, including building relationships	Listen attentively and respectfully, including habit of actively seeking feedback
Pro bono, community, bar association involvement	Analytical skills/law knowledge, including legal research	Commitment to firm/ department/company and its goals and values
Ability to work independently	Interview clients and witnesses	Effective communication skills, including oral and written
High quality work product, managing own work and multiple tasks (project management)	Initiates and maintains strong team and work relationships	Dedication to client service/ understanding of and responsiveness to client, including listening

6. Class Discussion: The Ten Critical Skills

a. The Big Reveal! The Ten Critical Skills Identified

Ten Critical Lawyering Skills

Instructions: Write out the ten critical lawyering skills below.	

b. Categorize the Ten Critical Skills

What do you notice about these critical skills? How would you categorize and group these ten critical skills?

To help you to answer these questions, please read the text boxes below.

> *"[S]uccessful entry-level lawyers are not merely legal technicians, nor are they merely cognitive powerhouses. New lawyers need some legal skills and require intelligence, but they are successful when they come to the job with a much broader blend of legal skills, professional competencies, and characteristics that comprise the whole lawyer."*[11]

> *"Historically, law schools send a message that success is only about grades and ranking; they do not clearly explain all of the competencies that legal employers and clients want and will assess."*[12]

---

11. Gerkman & Cornett, *supra* note 8, at 2.

12. Neil W. Hamilton, Roadmap: The Law Student's Guide To Meaningful Employment 17–18 (2023).

> *"The legal profession has never had a clear, explicit understanding of the minimum competence... lawyers need when they begin to practice law."*[13]

The ten critical lawyering skills identified above are the essence of this Workbook, class, and your professional identity. The remainder of this Workbook will focus on those skills that are otherwise generally not emphasized in the traditional law school curriculum.

13. Deborah Jones Merritt, *Building a Better Bar: The 12 Building Blocks of Minimum Competence*, IAALS (Oct. 28, 2020), https://iaals.du.edu/publications/building-better-bar.

2

Identifying and Demonstrating Your Lawyering Skills

LEARNING OUTCOMES

- Describe social competency for lawyers and explain your current competency level.
- Explain the process of identifying your top critical skills.
- List and summarize your top critical skills.
- Recognize and describe how critical skills and client service are connected.

Reflection: Part A & B

A final exam is one way for your professors to test or gauge your level of knowledge and engagement with the materials covered in class. This class, however, likely does not have a final exam. As such, alternative methods will test your engagement with the class material.

Part of your pre-class work for each chapter is designed to do just that. It is an alternative method to gauge your grasp of the chapter's learning objectives. Thus, each pre-class work module will always include the following two reflection exercises:

- Reflection Part A: Learning Objectives Self-Assessment
- Reflection Part B: Self-Directedness and Using Reflective Practice

Both of these exercises require you to self-assess your progress and learning from the previous class. Thus, each CLS chapter will begin with Reflection A and Reflection B, as identified above. You will find instructions for completing Reflection A: Learning Objectives Self-Assessment in the next table. Instructions for Reflection B: Using Reflective Practice, begins with the Pre-Class Work for chapter 3.

Reflection: Part A

Learning Objectives Self-Assessment

- To complete the following self-assessment exercise, read through the table below. The table lists the learning objectives from the previous chapter.
- If you can satisfy the objective, place a check mark in the box.
- If you do not understand the objective or if you have more questions about the objective, place a question mark in the box.

Note: When conducting a self-assessment, you always need solid evidence to support your choices. Here, your solid evidence is the ability to accomplish the stated learning objective.

AT THIS POINT, YOU SHOULD BE ABLE TO:	
	Recognize that lawyers often work in teams and partnerships.
	Explain and illustrate the importance of relying on solid, objective evidence in communicating professional identity and development.
	Name the top ten skills critical to a lawyer's professional identity.
	Explain what is meant by the term "the whole lawyer."

Identifying and Demonstrating Your Lawyering Skills

As you know, mastering the top ten skills identified in Chapter 1 is critical to helping form your professional identity. Practicing lawyers use those critical skills every day, and they are an important part of a practicing lawyer's everyday activities.

For litigation attorneys—whether they are in a courtroom, at a negotiation table, or reviewing discovery materials and evidence—these skills are indispensable in helping them manage their cases effectively, advocate for clients, and navigate the complexities of the legal system. For transactional attorneys, their daily activities often involve advising clients, drafting documents, negotiating deals, and ensuring compliance with laws and regulations. By applying these critical skills, non-litigation attorneys can effectively manage their clients' legal needs, facilitate business transactions, and ensure compliance with legal requirements.

Because mastering these skills is crucial to successfully practicing law, you must begin to identify and build these lawyering skills as you proceed down your professional identity path. You are probably already familiar with several of the skills that you have, use, and find particularly engaging/helpful. However, by entering law school, the context for the application of your existing skill set has changed.

The difference now is that you must learn and then consistently demonstrate the critical lawyering skills you identified in Chapter 1, first as a law student and next as a lawyer. The upshot is that this is the same skill set that legal employers and clients want and need. So, as you practice and master these skills, you will focus on what it means for you to be a lawyer while also becoming practice-ready for legal employers.

Pre-Class Work

1. Exercise: Strongest Skills Identification

You now have a solid foundation and understanding of the critical skills needed to serve both yourself as a lawyer and legal employers and clients. Within this framework, it is now time for you to identify *your* strongest skills as they relate to practicing law and the critical skills already identified.

Instructions:

- Complete the tables on the following pages. When asked to "demonstrate each of your strongest skills," remember that you are choosing from the critical skills identified in Chapter 1.
- For the sections that ask for "legal anecdotes," if you cannot list legal anecdotes, then list experiences either from law school or from outside of law school. These can be experiences that you have had or believe you may have in the near future.

Briefly describe two anecdotes in a *non-legal* context that demonstrate each of your strongest critical skills.		
	Anecdote 1	**Anecdote 2**
Critical Skill #1: ________ ________ ________ ________ ________ ________ ________ ________		
Critical Skill #2: ________ ________ ________ ________ ________ ________ ________ ________		
Critical Skill #3: ________ ________ ________ ________ ________ ________ ________ ________		

Briefly describe two anecdotes in a *legal* context that demonstrate each of your strongest critical skills.		
	Anecdote 1	**Anecdote 2**
Critical Skill #1: ________ ________ ________ ________ ________ ________ ________ ________		
Critical Skill #2: ________ ________ ________ ________ ________ ________ ________ ________		
Critical Skill #3: ________ ________ ________ ________ ________ ________ ________ ________		

2. Exercise: Identify Individual Critical Skills: Getting to Know Your Strengths

Now choose, list, and explain three of your *strongest* critical skills from the six you listed above. Please remember that your explanation must include the *solid evidence* (evidence legal employers would value) that you are relying upon to describe the skill as one of your top skills. If you do not have that solid evidence, *you must describe your plan for obtaining it* (which is an example of diagnosing your learning needs—another critical skill!).

My Strongest Skills	Explanation
Example 1 Initiative/drive/ strong work ethic	The solid evidence I am relying on to demonstrate this skill is the fact that I owned an ice cream store for four years before law school. I often worked eighty-hour weeks. I taught myself how to run a small business, including bookkeeping, taxes, marketing, managing employees, and customer service.
Example 2 Commitment to firm/department and its goals and values	I do not currently have solid evidence to demonstrate this skill. I did not think of it before this exercise. However, my plan for obtaining it is that since I am a currently a member of the Black Law Student Association (BLSA) at my law school, I will run for 2L representative. I will also plan to run for a board position (president or vice president). I will find out when and how to apply for these positions. This will demonstrate a commitment to BLSA and its goals and values. This same commitment is easily transferable to any legal department to which I have a genuine interest and will soon apply.
1.	
2.	
3.	

3. Reflective Learning: Professional Development and Self-Directedness

Because rubrics offer a range of benefits—like providing clear criteria for performance and encouraging reflective thinking—CLS makes good use of them. Below is a *Professional Development and Self-Directedness*[1] rubric that you will use to complete the next exercise.

For now, however, you will first focus on using this rubric to learn how to demonstrate the "commitment to and pursuit of professional development and self-directed learning" critical skill.

No matter what type of professional or non-professional experience you already have, your job as a law student is to build your professional identity and move toward becoming a practice-ready lawyer. Becoming practice ready is specific and defined, and you must demonstrate (with solid evidence) the critical skills that help characterize this movement (movement from law student to lawyer).

Professional development and self-directedness is one of those critical skills. The rubric below specifically defines what it means—giving you the opportunity to objectively measure your current developmental level, understand the actions you need to take to progress, and keep track of your progress as you gain experience.

You can think of rubrics as a way to help you **Map—Move—Measure™** your professional identity progress. The goal is to progress along the rubrics in CLS so that you have the solid evidence you need to both communicate these critical skills and demonstrate your growing mastery of these skills to legal employers.

Thus, in this class, two items are always important: (1) building your professional identity as you move from student to lawyer, and (2) objectively measuring and communicating that movement with solid evidence. The following rubric will help you do both, and you will revisit this rubric throughout the course. Take some time now and review the *Self-Directedness* rubric on the following page.

Remember, it is one thing to say that you have improved and gained experience, but it is something else to demonstrate that improvement with solid evidence.

Moving along this rubric will provide concrete examples (solid evidence) of your self-directedness. In effect, this rubric will help you to quantify the professional development and self-directedness critical skill. It will give you both the map you need so you know how to improve that critical skill and the ability to measure your progress as you move toward eventual mastery as a practicing lawyer.

---

1. Holloran Center for Ethical Leadership, *Self-Directedness Milestone*, UNIVERSITY OF ST. THOMAS, https://law.stthomas.edu/about/centers-institutes/holloran-center/competency-milestones/self-directedness/index.html (competency milestones database) (last visited Dec. 2, 2024).

Rubric: Assessment of Student's Ownership of Continuous Professional Development (Self-Directedness)

Sub-Competencies of Ownership/ Self-Directedness	Novice Learner (Level 1)	Intermediate Learner (Level2)	Competent Learner (Level 3)	Exceptional Learner (Level 4)
1. Self-Assesses and Identifies Strengths and Areas for Growth *Understands full range of lawyering competencies and diagnoses learning needs*	RARELY demonstrates understanding of full range of lawyering competencies and diagnoses learning needs	SOMETIMES demonstrates understanding of full range of lawyering competencies and diagnoses learning needs	OFTEN demonstrates understanding of full range of lawyering competencies and diagnoses learning needs	CONSISTENTLY demonstrates understanding of full range of lawyering competencies and diagnoses learning needs
2. Articulates Goals and Follows a Plan *Implements a written professional development plan reflecting goals that are specific, measurable, achievable, relevant, and time-bound*	RARELY creates and implements a written professional development plan reflecting goals that are specific, measurable, achievable, relevant, and time-bound	SOMETIMES creates and implements a written professional development plan reflecting goals that are specific, measurable, achievable, relevant, and time-bound	OFTEN creates and implements a written professional development plan reflecting goals that are specific, measurable, achievable, relevant, and time-bound	CONSISTENTLY creates and implements a written professional development plan reflecting goals that are specific, measurable, achievable, relevant, and time-bound
3. Acquires and Learns from Experience *Seeks experiences to develop competencies and meet articulated goals, and seeks and incorporates feedback received during the experiences*	RARELY seeks experiences or seeks and incorporates feedback received during the experiences	SOMETIMES seeks experiences and seeks and incorporates feedback received during the experiences	OFTEN seeks experiences and seeks and incorporates feedback received during the experiences	CONSISTENTLY seeks experiences and seeks and incorporates feedback received during the experiences
4. Reflects and Applies Lessons Learned *Uses reflective practice to reflect on performance, contemplate lessons learned, identify how to apply lessons learned to improve in the future, and applies those lessons*	RARELY uses reflective practice to reflect on performance, contemplate lessons learned, identify how to apply lessons learned to improve in the future, and applies those lessons	SOMETIMES uses reflective practice to reflect on performance, contemplate lessons learned, identify how to apply lessons learned to improve in the future, and applies those lessons	OFTEN uses reflective practice to reflect on performance, contemplate lessons learned, identify how to apply lessons learned to improve in the future, and applies those lessons	CONSISTENTLY uses reflective practice to reflect on performance, contemplate lessons learned, identify how to apply lessons learned to improve in the future, and applies those lessons

4. Exercise: Demonstrating Lawyering Skills

Instructions:

- For this exercise you will focus on the sub-competency in the first column, *Self-Assesses and Identifies Strengths and Areas for Growth*.
- You will note that part of measuring this competency requires you to diagnose your own learning needs. What does that mean?
- Diagnosing your own learning needs means you identify the gaps in your knowledge, skills, and behaviors. It is a process of self-assessment and reflection that helps you understand what you need to learn or improve upon to achieve your professional goals. Diagnosing your own learning needs is similar to problem solving (also a critical skill), but it is solely focused on identifying your individual knowledge gaps.
- Because this is the first rubric tied to Pre-Class Work, you will find a broader definition of the column-one sub-competency below.

Self-Assesses and Identifies Strengths and Areas of Growth

Sub-Competencies of Ownership/ Self-Directedness	Novice Student (Level 1)	Advanced Beginner (Level 2)	Intermediate (Level 3)	Student at Graduation (Level 4)	Junior Attorney (Level 5)
1. Self-Assesses and Identifies Strengths and Areas for Growth Understands full range of competencies legal employers and clients want and diagnoses learning needs	Expects faculty/staff to identify student's goals. Limits engagement to tasks assigned by faculty in graded courses. Rarely seeks to independently understand the full range of competencies legal employers and clients want.	Occasionally seeks to understand the competencies needed by legal employers and clients and how student's strengths fit with those needs. Takes initial steps toward reaching student's goals by diagnosing learning needs and resources available to reach them. Begins to see value in non-graded opportunities.	Regularly seeks to understand the competencies needed by legal employers and how student's strengths fit with those needs. Student is in process of taking ownership over the path to reach student's goals by employing appropriate resources to meet learning needs. Sees value in non-graded opportunities.	Understands the competencies that clients and legal employers need and how student's strengths fit with those needs. Tries to understand and anticipate senior lawyers' and clients' wider context/business needs. Takes full ownership over the path to reach student's goals by creatively seeking resources to meet learning needs.	Meets Student at Graduation criteria (Level 4) and, in addition, is proactively learning: (1) how clients consume legal services and why and when legal services are needed by clients; (2) the business of law and how to provide better service to the employer; and (3) the competencies that practice experience now makes clear are needed.

a. Reflecting and Assessing Your Individual Top Skills

In this section, you are using the *Self-Assesses and Identifies Strengths and Areas of Growth* rubric in relation to the top strengths/skills exercise that you completed above. It is now time for you to reflect and diagnose your learning needs in order to map and measure your progress in objectively improving this critical skill, and you are going to first focus on improving your top strengths/skills.

Instructions:

- From the above Exercise: Identify Individual Critical Skills: Getting to Know Your Strengths, select one of the skills you listed and copy it in the first row of the table below.
- Next, review the rubric, moving across the column from left to right. And with your chosen top skill/strength in mind, choose which level to slot yourself given both the level of detail you provided and the application of your chosen skill/strength.
- Circle your level of development in the left column in the table below. Then, in the space provided, provide the solid, objective evidence you are relying upon in making that choice. In other words, in making your selection, state the following: "This is the level I chose because I have the following solid evidence to support that choice."

Example

<table>
<tr><td>NOVICE STUDENT</td><td rowspan="5">I chose Novice Student because I have the following solid evidence to support that choice.
I have yet to reach Level 2 (but I will get there before mid-semester!). I never knew anything about competencies (never used that language) before this class. I rarely attend any law school panels or events. I do not have a good understanding or knowledge about law school organizations, the career office, etc. I also have not figured out the learning needs piece.</td></tr>
<tr><td>Advanced Beginner</td></tr>
<tr><td>Intermediate</td></tr>
<tr><td>Student at Graduation</td></tr>
<tr><td>Junior Attorney</td></tr>
</table>

Your Turn

Top Skill/Strength	
Novice Student	
Advanced Beginner	
Intermediate	
Student at Graduation	
Junior Attorney	

5. Social Competence: An Expanded Definition of Cultural Competence

a. Why Social Competence?

Cultural competence is not listed as a top critical lawyering skill. In fact, cultural competence did not make the critical-skills list in Chapter 1. Nevertheless, there is no doubt that it is a critical skill; the problem is that the current framing is too narrow. Social competence, which includes cultural competence, provides better framing because it expands the definition, truly capturing the skill lawyers use and need.

First, as far as cultural competence is concerned, the legal profession has traditionally placed little emphasis on cultural competence or diversity training for law students or lawyers.[2] And although the call to diversity and belonging in the legal profession has always had a voice, recently that voice has gotten louder.

---

2. Debra Chopp, *Addressing Cultural Bias in the Legal Profession*, 41 NYU Rev. L. & Soc. Change 367, 369 (2017), https://repository.law.umich.edu/cgi/viewcontent.cgi?article=2874&context=articles.

The main accreditation body for most American law schools, for example, recently mandated that law schools "provide education to law students on bias, cross-cultural competency, and racism."[3]

In spite of this new recognition, however, the current and most common narratives advocating for culturally competent lawyers fails, and cultural competence rarely bubbles to the top of any survey measuring critical lawyering skills. Why? Because "culturally competent" lawyering fails to link to the social competence that all law students must develop and all lawyers need.

b. The Failure of Cultural Competence

The current narrative for why lawyers should focus on developing cultural competence chiefly travels in two untenable lanes of argument: lane one says that lawyers "should" become culturally competent because it is the right thing to do, and lane two says that lawyers "need" cultural competence to successfully navigate the realities of practicing law and working within a diverse profession.

Those two arguments are best summarized as a morality and a practice-necessity argument, respectively. Below are examples of the typical framing of these two arguments:

"Lawyers today practice in an increasingly diverse society...."[4]	Practice necessity
"Becoming culturally competent is important, not only because it is the right thing to do, but also because inevitably it will affect the attorney's business...."[5]	Moral argument and Practice necessity
"Cultural competency is key for lawyers to effectively serve and gain the trust of their clients...."[6]	Practice necessity
"[B]eyond the client context, attorneys also encounter many different cultures when interacting with coworkers, other firms, opposing counsel[, and] judges."[7]	Practice necessity

---

3. ABA Standards and Rules of Procedure for Approval of Law Schools 2023–2024, https://www.americanbar.org/content/dam/aba/administrative/legal_education_and_admissions_to_the_bar/standards/2023-2024/23-24-standards-ch3.pdf.

4. *Id.* at 368.

5. Aastha Madaan, *Cultural Competency and the* Practice of Law in the 21st Century, ABA J. (Mar. 1, 2017), https://www.americanbar.org/groups/real_property_trust_estate/publications/probate-property-magazine/2016/march_april_2016/2016_aba_rpte_pp_v30_2_article_madaan_cultural_competency_and_the_practice_of_law_in_the_21st_century/.

6. Neil W. Hamilton, Roadmap: The Law Student's Guide to Meaningful Employment 166 (*2d e*d. 2018).

7. Id.

However, as you will see below, the existing data and practice demographics makes framing cultural competence in this manner impractical. The reality is that, under this framework, most lawyers in the United States today simply do not need to be or become culturally competent.

c. Debunking the Morality Argument

Let us look more closely at the morality argument, which imposes a moral obligation on lawyers to become culturally competent. This argument proves difficult at best because it effectively relies on a "shaming" component to encourage behavior change. By arguing that lawyers "have to," "need to," or simply "should" become culturally competent, this argument dictates the outcome while overlooking the process.

It is well established, however, that changing one's behavior is not a simple process, and that shaming or dictating behavior change is rarely effective. Indeed, this approach has done little to effectuate any cultural change within the legal profession: cultural competence rarely rises in the rankings of lawyering practice/skills surveys. It is a critical skill that is notable for its consistent inclusion failure.

d. Debunking the Practice-Necessity Argument

In 2018, the ABA reported the following statistics for attorneys:[8]

Percentage of Attorneys Who Identify As:

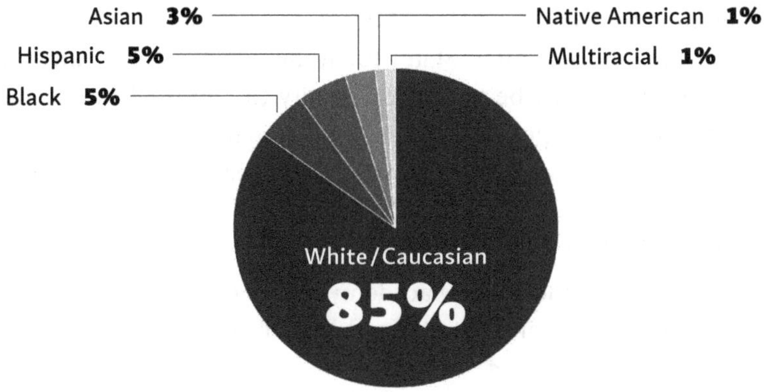

Thus, despite cultural competence being framed as a "practice necessity" in navigating legal work, we can easily see that most lawyers in the United States will neither work with nor for lawyers whose dominant culture is different from their own. But what about clients? Is having cultural competence imperative for lawyers to successfully navigate and represent clients?

8. Debra Cassens Weiss, *Lawyer Population 15% Higher than 10 Years Ago, New ABA Data Shows*, ABA J. (May 3, 2018, 2:13 PM CDT), https://www.abajournal.com/news/article/lawyer_population_15_higher_than_10_years_ago_new_aba_data_shows.

Although it is difficult to find accurate data on the demographic makeup of clients, we do know that most people who actually need legal representation in the United States simply cannot afford it. As *Newsweek* noted in 2024, "average lawyer hourly rates run from $211 to $424 . . . [t]his puts legal help far out of reach for the average American, who has a median income of $74,580, according to the U.S. Census Bureau."[9]

Indeed, Gillian Hadfield, a law professor and economist at the University of Toronto, has noted that "well over 80% of Americans who need legal help can't get it because it's too expensive."[10]

Thus, most lawyers in the United States represent a very small percentage of the population: those who can afford legal services. When we consider that, according to the 2020 U.S. census, 61.6 percent of the U.S. population identified as "white American," along with the reality that the vast majority of wealth in the United States is owned by white Americans,[11] it is also true that most lawyers will represent clients who are, by majority, white. In other words, most lawyers in the United States will never represent a client who is not white.

This is not to suggest that there is no diversity in the lawyering profession. For example, as the author of this book, I teach at a law school that is consistently recognized as one of the most diverse law schools in the country.[12] It may well be that, if you attend a diverse law school or live in a socially diverse area, developing your cultural competence skill set is indeed the right thing and the practice-necessary thing to do.

Notwithstanding, this representation of diversity is simply not true for most law students and lawyers in the United States today. So, while the morality and practice-necessity arguments may be a practical reality to a limited extent, neither of these viewpoints alone will persuade legal professionals to develop their cultural competence based on existing data, evidence and the reality of practicing law.

e. Social Competence as a Critical Lawyering Skill

In light of this, lawyers and the law academy must begin to ask a different question. Given the general lack of diversity in the legal profession and in the clients

---

9. Suzanne Blake, *Middle-Class Americans Can't Afford to Lawyer Up*, NEWSWEEK (Jan. 24, 2024, 8:01 PM EST), https://www.newsweek.com/middle-class-afford-lawyer-fees-legal-help-1863747.

10. Greg Rosalsky, *Most People Can't Afford Legal Help. 1 Reformer Wants to Change That*, PLANET MONEY (Sep. 29, 2020, 9:35 AM ET), https://www.npr.org/sections/money/2020/09/29/917824026/most-people-cant-afford-legal-help-1-reformer-wants-to-change-that.

11. *King's Dream Remains an Elusive Goal; Many Americans See Racial Disparities*, PEW RES. CTR. (Aug. 22, 2013), https://www.pewsocialtrends.org/2013/08/22/kings-dream-remains-an-elusive-goal-many-americans-see-racial-disparities/.

12. *2023 Class Profile*, SANTA CLARA UNIV. SCH. OF LAW, https://law.scu.edu/admissions/2023-class-profile/.

served, why should law students and lawyers care about being culturally competent? Put another way, why is cultural competence a critical lawyering skill?

Cultural competence is a critical lawyering skill because it will help *all* lawyers serve and better understand each other and *all* clients—even given the current homogeneous environment in which most lawyers practice.

If empathy "is at the heart of developing cross-cultural competency," and "is the ability to walk in another person's shoes, to view life from his or her perspective, and to communicate that understanding and an intention to help," and "is demonstrated by active listening,"[13] then the critical skills that were identified in Chapter 1 are clearly applicable to developing cultural competence.

The following table demonstrates the interdependence between critical lawyering skills, your professional identity, and cultural competence. You will recognize the skills listed in the second column from Chapter 1: with "S/Z" standing for the Shultz/Zedeck survey and "FFP" for the Foundations for Practice survey.

Competencies Necessary for Cultural Competence	Competencies Necessary for Professional Identity Formation
Advance the client's interests	Provide advice and counsel and building relationships with clients **(S/Z)**
Work with adversaries and decision makers whom the lawyer seeks to influence	Develop relationships within the legal profession **(S/Z)**
Empathy	Demonstrate tolerance, sensitivity, and compassion; treat others with courtesy and respect **(FFP)**
The ability to walk in another person's shoes	See the world through the eyes of others **(S/Z)**
Communicate understanding and an intention to help	Work cooperatively and collaboratively as part of a team **(FFP)**
Active listening	Listen attentively and respectfully **(FFP)**

See the synergy? Mastering these critical skills as you develop your professional identity will also equip you to move toward social competence.

13. Hamilton, *supra* note 6.

f. Social Competence as Better Framing

Because social competence better captures how lawyers use the critical skills noted above, and because it also includes cultural competence, it is the better term to use here.

The critical skills noted above apply to all of the populations a lawyer may work with, whether neurotypical or neurodivergent; heterosexual, cisgender, or LGBTQ+; wealthy or poor; white or BIPOC; and so on.

The current framing does a grave injustice by limiting the competency to "culture." In short, law students must develop social competence, and mastering the critical skills already identified is the path that will get you there.

Mastering the top critical lawyering skills as you build your professional identity will also increase your social (and cultural) competence. Lawyers who understand and are sensitive to social differences are lawyers who embody professionalism and competence. In other words, your path to professional identity includes mastering the same skills you need on your path to becoming socially and culturally competent.

g. Conclusion

You are thus uniquely equipped to be, or to become, socially competent by focusing on your professional identity. Working to increase your critical skills will also help increase your social competence, and vice versa.

Finally, if we believe that lawyers do indeed have a moral and practice imperative, then it should be directed toward improving access to the law. After all, lawyers are the stewards of the administration of law and legal justice in the United States. Social competence includes and goes far beyond the lawyer's business and work environment. It should also include empathy toward those who currently cannot afford legal services.

If lawyers do not take this responsibility and improve their own profession and promote access to justice, who will? And when? So, there may be room for moral and practice components after all. Because fixing our profession and promoting access to justice is indeed the right thing to do.

6. Exercise: Social Competency: Part A

This exercise has two parts. You will complete Part A now. You will need to complete Part A in order to complete Part B. Part B is due in Chapter 4. Thus, you *must* complete this Part A activity before your Chapter 4 Pre-Class Work is due.

Instructions:

Review the Cultural Competency Milestone below, paying particular attention to the last column (Examples of Statements a Person in this Stage Might Make).

Cultural Competency Milestone[14]

Stage of Cultural Competence	Description of Knowledge, Behaviors, and Values	Examples of Statements a Person in this Stage Might Make
Chauvinism about a Particular Culture	I recognize broad, general categories of culture. But not only do I believe that my culture is superior to other cultures, I believe that members of other cultures have no or only a limited place/role in my community.	• Women don't have the ability to do math and science the way men do. • Brown and Black people are on every street corner, selling their babies for drugs. • Whites are just smarter than other people. • You're taking a seat meant for an able-bodied student. • Foreign students come here to have U.S.-born anchor babies. • Affirmative action is stopping Asian Americans from being accepted in law school based on merit.
Unawareness of Cultural Differences	I don't have personal assumptions and biases based on culture. I may recognize broad, general categories such as "foreigners," "gays," and "people of color." I prefer to be with people who are like me.	• I don't have a culture. • People are different because of personality, intelligence, or experience. • I treat everyone—students, faculty, staff, clients—the same. • I spoke with John and Jack (fellow white male faculty) before the meeting, and they agree that we don't need a diversity proposal. • I don't understand why the students of color don't volunteer as much in my class. • I find it more satisfying and effective to work in a group of people like me.

continued

14. *Cultural Competency Milestone*, Univ. of St. Thomas Sch. of Law, https://law.stthomas.edu/about/centers-institutes/holloran-center/competency-milestones/cultural-competency/index.html (last visited Sep. 9, 2024).

continued

Preference for a Particular Culture	I know there are other cultures, but my culture is better than other cultures. Other cultures just aren't as moral. I sort people by whether they belong to my culture or not. OR I think another culture is better than mine. So, I try to belong to that culture.	• This is America. Everyone should speak English and accept Jesus Christ as their savior. • Immigrants are changing our country too much. • People in other countries should try to be more like us. • We do not want to change our law school's culture; we need students/faculty who are the right "fit." • Law school is hard; women and students of color have trouble making it. • Like the United States, our law school is a melting pot. • Americans abroad are so embarrassing. I try to hang out only with the locals.
Minimization of Cultural Difference	I believe that cultural differences are superficial, like food, music, and clothing. All people share universal human traits and values (like the ones at the heart of my culture). Because we are all the same inside, I act like myself, no matter who I'm with, and I treat everyone the same. In my country, I don't believe that anyone has an advantage due to culture.	• There are some differences in the details, but human values are universal. • People are really all the same inside. • Everyone has an equal opportunity to make it in this country. • There is nothing special about culturally competent lawyering; clients simply need good lawyers. • We [admit students/hire faculty] based on merit; we are not going to lower our standards. • Cultural intolerance does not explain the problems women and students of color have; they just need to work harder. • Writing about race/gender/LGBTQ+/faith/poverty/etc. is not "real" scholarship; serving on committees dedicated to diversity issues is not a serious contribution to the school. • I do not see a need to adjust my teaching methods to be more inclusive because cultural differences are exaggerated; good students will always do well.

Appreciation of Cultural Differences and Acknowledgment of Cultural Diversity/ Equity	I believe that all behaviors and values, including my own, are constructed in distinct and observable cultural contexts that are equally authentic human experiences (cultural relativism). I try to understand how general cultural context and patterns affect my own and other people's specific behavior and values. That doesn't mean that I agree with or prefer another culture's values. Rather, I try not to judge another culture based on my own culture's values, even when I don't like the behavior or value of the other culture. Sometimes, trying to be nonjudgmental can feel as though I'm not being true to my own cultural values. Being aware of general cultural context and patterns means I have to be careful to focus on the specific people I'm interacting with. I try not to expect them to follow all the general values and behaviors of their culture. I know that systematic privilege for dominant cultural groups exists. If I'm a member of a dominant group or in a role that gives me power or authority over someone who is different from myself, I try to be careful about how I act. I don't want to be blind to privilege or seem as though I'm judging their culture. I don't want to offend someone else.	• When I travel or study abroad, I try to learn about the culture of the country I'm going to. • I try to learn about the cultures of my colleagues/clients/adversaries so that I can better understand their perspectives. • When I saw how my client addressed his wife, I believed she didn't mind, as I know their home country is more patriarchal than ours. But I worried that my unconscious body language made me look as though I was judging them. • I believe it is important for my students to develop culturally competent lawyering skills. • I know students have raised concerns about diversity/inclusion, but I do not feel that I am the right person to address those concerns. I have no credibility because I am white/male/ straight/etc. • I try to get to know each of my students as individuals and learn about their cultural backgrounds. • We celebrate the diversity of our school through various events such as Black History Month and Women's History Month. • I recognize the course text may not be effective at including issues of race/ gender/LGBTQ+/faith/poverty/etc., but I do not feel empowered to discuss these issues in class myself. • I know we have faculty who write about race/gender/LGBTQ+/faith/ poverty/etc., but I do not feel equipped to digest that scholarship.

continued

continued

Responsiveness to Cultural Differences/ Diversity/Inclusion	I learn about cultural differences before working with others, including by seeking out cultural informants and researching cultural differences. I consciously shift my perspective and behavior in response to another's culture. That means I practice empathy, withholding judgment, and cultural frame-of-reference shifting in working with others. I use tools such as The Five Habits of Cross-Cultural Lawyering. I am motivated to practice because, the more I practice, the more fluid and authentic my adaptations become, and the more effective I become in making an experience more culturally accessible for other people. I apply my own cultural and professional values in culturally relative ways.	• To work with these opposing lawyers, I have to remember that their culture is more status-oriented; so I have to use their titles and ask for permission more often. • When I schedule meetings with clients who are religious, I pay attention to their days of worship and holidays. • I'm beginning to feel that I can maintain my own values and still work effectively in this law firm. • The more I understand this culture, the better I get at following their jokes. • I recognize that I must be a culturally competent legal educator in order to cultivate culturally competent lawyering skills in my students. • I try to get to know each of my students as individuals and learn about their cultural backgrounds. I am trying to be more inclusive in my teaching methods. • I understand that the cultural background of my students may affect their experience in law school; when faced with a concern, I try to be an ally. • I participate in the cultural celebrations in the law school (e.g., Women's History Month) but realize inclusivity requires a deeper commitment. • One of my priorities in choosing a course text is how well the text incorporates issues of race/gender/ LGBTQ+/ faith/ poverty/etc.

Fluency in Cultural Inclusion	I see all people as culturally unique because we each create our own cultural and personal identities, based on the more general cultural contexts and patterns that we experience. I like being able to integrate the different cultures that I belong to into a positive whole. I use power in culturally appropriate ways, with an emphasis on reconciling differences. I look for and create opportunities for multicultural interactions. I support others in creating their own multicultural or intersectional identities.	• I am a better interviewer because I can draw on different cultural frames of reference. • I am comfortable working in teams. I enjoy finding cultural connections to and among all the members, even when some differences seem to outweigh similarities. • I like that in this community newcomers and existing residents work together to continuously change our community to fit all of us. • I recognize that faith and science can be compatible. • I enjoy having students from different backgrounds in class because diversity enriches classroom discussion. • I am learning how to handle conflicts or disagreements that may arise during class instead of dismissing or cutting off the discussion. • Having more students of different races, genders, sexual orientations, faiths, socio-economic statuses, etc. is better for our school, and I prioritize the work it takes to maintain an inclusive environment. • I am committed to the continuing work of cultural competence and know that it will be a lifelong journey of learning for me and my students.
1. Choose your current "Stage of Competence" from the first row and write it into the Reflection Dashboard below.		
2. Now think about the stage you chose. Why did you choose it? Write your answer to that question in the table below.		

Reflection Dashboard

What developmental level are you at now?
Stage of Competence:
I chose this stage because...(your description here will apply to your personal experiences):

Participate in an Activity

How will you continue to grow and expand your social competence, of which cultural competence is a part? Remember, cultural competence incorporates those critical lawyering skills that help define your professional identity formation; the skill set for cultural competence is the same skill set needed for social competence and professional identity.

For this exercise, you are going to identify an activity and the specific steps you will take to complete that activity. You must remember to think broadly. If you do not stretch yourself beyond your current environment, it is unlikely that you will succeed in moving toward mastery on your professional identity journey.

The following list includes some suggested activities. The goal is to identify a diverse topic on which you will focus and engage several critical skills. This list is not exhaustive, by any means.

- ▹ Attend a law school event sponsored by a cultural organization different from your own.
- ▹ Attend a local bar association event sponsored or centered on a culture different from your own.
- ▹ Watch a diverse TED Talk or TEDx Talk.
- ▹ Watch a diverse documentary or film.

- Select an article to read that is centered on diversity/cultural competence.
- Attend an online lecture or take an online training regarding diversity and inclusion, cultural diversity, etc.

Select and write out your chosen activity in the next table. You will use what you learn from your activity to complete your Chapter 4 Pre-Class Work. Again, you must complete this activity before your Chapter 4 Pre-Class Work is due.

Please also provide *specific* information regarding the date and venue, website, name of article, etc., along with a brief summary for your chosen selection, and include that information in the following table.

Note: Your description must be specific enough to allow your professor to Google or otherwise locate the activity.

My chosen activity is:	
Brief summary of the activity:	
The three skills I expect to focus on to complete this activity are:	
1	
2	
3	
I will complete this activity by (date *must* be prior to Chapter 4):	

Good luck and have fun! Remember, this is a safe space in which to explore and learn about a new topic while, at the same time, actively engaging with the critical skills that will help you become a better lawyer.

Pre-Class Work Complete

In-Class Activity

1. Class Discussion: Review of Chapter 1

Measuring Learning Objectives (Self-Assessment): Questions and comments

2. Class Discussion: Social Competence

We will discuss the Pre-Class Work assignment and reading.

3. Class Discussion: Analyze and Discuss Top Skills within Overall List

Explain the process of identifying and defining your strongest skills/competencies.

4. Class Activity and Discussion: Role-Plays and Scenarios

Critical Skill: Dedication to Client Service/Understanding of and Responsiveness to Client, Including Promptly Responding to Inquiries and Requests

> Note: All material for the scenarios and role-plays in this class are actual scenarios that happened to either the author, Thiadora Pina, or her friends when they were first-year or second-year lawyers.
>
> The only exception is the role-play for Chapter 4, which was developed by attorney Laura Jacobus, who has led multiple legal organizations in high-tech companies, including Ethics and Compliance, Legal Operations, and Global Transactions. The Chapter 4 scenario is typical of the way an in-house corporate legal department works.

Role-Play: Sam and the Phone Call

Instructions:

- Choose a partner. One of you will be the lawyer and the other will be the client (you will switch roles in a later class).
- Read through *only* your part of the scenario. Then, role-play and have a conversation.
- After working through the scenario, work together to write out answers to the questions that follow. Good luck!

Role-Play Lawyer:

You receive a call from Sam, one of your long-time clients, whom you have gotten to know well over the many years you have represented Sam. Sam owns several small businesses for which you first prepared the start-up paperwork. You continue to act as legal counsel for the businesses' myriad ongoing legal issues, from employment issues to permitting, etc. Sam has been a very good client for years. Sam is also a very good referral source and has sent additional clients and business your way throughout the years.

On this day, you're busy preparing for a trial that starts next week. Your assistant knows not to interrupt you when you're in the "war room," but your assistant puts through a phone call from Sam because Sam tells your assistant "to get my lawyer on the phone right away!" You're annoyed at the interruption, but because Sam is calling, you take the call.

You pick up the phone and say. . .

Role-Play Lawyer:

Background Information about Sam's Concern:
The state where you practice and where Sam resides is not a common law marriage state. The expectation of being married someday is not actionable. There is no cause of action for what Sam is asking you to do.

After speaking with Sam, you must give Sam an answer/explanation. You do not need to do any research into this matter. You know that Sam's issue is not actionable.

Role-Play Client:

Your name is Sam. You are a successful entrepreneur, and you have known and trusted your lawyer for years. You and your partner recently broke up. Your partner was a *very* successful entrepreneur, and their business was recently acquired by Meta, Inc. Your partner has way more money than you. You lived together for eight years, and you always expected you would eventually be married, but now your partner has left you. You could not be more upset! You want legal recourse. You are going to sue them!!

You pick up the phone and call to speak with your lawyer. You own several small businesses for which your lawyer prepared the startup paperwork. Your lawyer continues to act as legal counsel for the myriad ongoing legal issues your businesses deal with on a daily basis, from employment issues, to permitting, etc. You've been a very good client for years. You've also been a very good referral source, and you have sent additional clients and business to your lawyer throughout the years. You know your lawyer well.

When you call your lawyer's office, your lawyer's assistant tells you that your lawyer can't come to the phone. You're really upset about this whole situation. You did not see it coming! You tell the assistant that you don't care how busy your lawyer is— "I need to speak to my lawyer right away!"

Your lawyer picks up the phone, and...

- Name, define, and describe some of the skills you just worked through. Be sure to also connect each skill to the relevant part of the story.

Skill	Description

Role-Play and Scenario: The Big Box Store

Critical Skill: Dedication to Client Service/Understanding of and Responsiveness to Client, Including Promptly Responding to Inquiries and Requests

Scenario: The Big Box Store

Instructions:

1. Choose a partner—for this scenario, you will work together.
2. Read through the scenario, and then work together to write out answers to the questions that follow. Good luck!

Your firm was hired to prosecute a personal injury action. Your client, Maria, fell at The Big Box Store as she was walking to the bathroom. Your client broke her ankle and required two separate surgeries to repair the damage. At the time, your client was a high-level executive consultant and travelled frequently for work. She missed several weeks of work due to the injury and the resulting rehabilitation. Because she worked as an independent contractor, she did not receive any wages during the time she could not work. The case was assigned to you.

You first read the case file and then place a call to Maria. You introduce yourself and answer her questions about the case. You also tell Maria about your thoughts and strategy regarding the case, and you let her know that you'll be available to answer her questions. Because the case file was thin, you also have quite a few questions for her. Going through your long list of questions is going to take some time, so after you ask if she has any more questions, you tell her that you're going to transfer the call to your assistant to take down some more information about the case. Your assistant is great at working with your clients, and together, you've already gone over the information you need and want to find out. You tell Maria that you'll talk to her soon, and then you transfer the call.

About two weeks later, you are combing through the file and going over the information your assistant took down. You are grateful because your assistant typed up the notes and did a great job getting the information you wanted. After you review the file, you place a call to Maria, with whom you haven't spoken in about two weeks. You give her an update on the case, answer all her questions, and let her know that you'll call her again in a couple of weeks. This is pretty much the schedule you keep after first checking with Maria, and Maria said it is fine with her. In general, you are good at updating and answering all of your client's questions.

Eventually, through your investigation, you find out that The Big Box Store was in violation of relevant codes. The floor leading to the store's restrooms has a 3 percent rise even though the applicable code clearly states that any rise in flooring greater than 2 percent requires a railing and clearly marked signs indicating the rise. Neither of these requirements was met at The Big Box Store at the time your client fell.

After you uncover these findings—which took a significant amount of effort on your part—you draft a demand letter to The Big Box Store. After several phone calls with The Big Box Store and approval from your client, you finally settle the case. You settle the case for a significant amount (full value), recovering lost wages, medical expenses, pain and suffering, and future medical payments. Your client and the firm's managing partners are thrilled with the settlement amount.

- Question: Did you provide excellent client service? Why or why not?
- Be sure to specifically name the applicable competencies.

Yes, excellent client service	No, client service was lacking

5. Class Discussion: Skill Identification

- Debrief scenarios.
- Identify and describe at least four skills from the list of lawyering skills provided in Chapter 1 that were or could/should have been demonstrated in the scenario.

Skill	How Demonstrated

3 Aligning Your Interests to Your Personal Identity

LEARNING OUTCOMES

- Describe the self-directed competency of "reflective practice" and illustrate its relation to your professional identity.
- Identify your top interests.
- Summarize why utilizing interests matters in professional identity formation.
- Explain the link between utilizing interests, wellness, and professional identity.
- Demonstrate concrete examples of different ways law school supports finding and utilizing your interests.
- Identify some ways attorneys and legal employers flag the interests and skills they find necessary in future employees.
- Explain the term "growth mindset" and apply it to a personal anecdote.

Reflection: Part A

Learning Objectives Self-Assessment

- To complete the following self-assessment exercise, read through the table below. The table lists the learning objectives from the previous chapter.
- If you can satisfy the objective, place a check mark in the box.
- If you do not understand the objective or if you have more questions about the objective, place a question mark in the box.

Note: You need solid evidence to support your choices. Here, your solid evidence is the ability to accomplish the stated learning objective.

AT THIS POINT, YOU SHOULD BE ABLE TO:	
	Describe social competency for lawyers and explain your current competency level.
	Explain the process of identifying your top critical skills.
	List and summarize your top critical skills.
	Recognize and describe how critical skills and client service are connected.

Reflection: Part B

Self-Directedness and Using Reflective Practice: Top Competencies/Skills

The following rubric focuses on the self-directed competency of "reflective practice." In lieu of a final exam, you will utilize this rubric and method to test your knowledge and engagement with the class material.

Professor Lisle Baker notes that "[o]ne aspect of professionalism is the idea that learning is lifelong, and that mastery comes from sustained efforts at self-development over time."[1]

---

1. R. Lisle Baker, *Designing a Positive Psychology Course for Lawyers*, 51 SUFFOLK U. L. REV. 207, 244 (2018), https://ssrn.com/abstract=3271713. Thiadora Pina is indebted to R. Lisle Baker for providing this paper.

The practice of reflection means that you purposely think about the adjustments you need to make; you do not simply apply the same tools to the same task. In studying and using reflective practice, you are simply naming and bringing your focused attention to a skill or habit that you already engage in when you want to get better and improve at something—be it learning to play guitar or being a lawyer.

In this class, as you know, two items are always important: (1) building your professional identity as you move from student to lawyer, and (2) objectively measuring and communicating that movement with solid evidence. The following rubric will help you do both.

You will use the rubric that is described in the next table throughout your remaining time using CLS and (hopefully) beyond. You will find this Reflection: Part B assignment in each of the following chapters. After each chapter, you will be asked to demonstrate solid professional development by purposely engaging in and tracking your reflective practice for that chapter. The solid evidence you will rely upon will vary, depending on what it is that is being measured.

With respect to Chapter 2 and your top competencies, you will rely on the anecdotes from the Chapter 2 Pre-Class Work. One example of working through and using this rubric looks like this:

Using Reflective Practice: Top Competencies/Skills

Step 1	**Reflect** ▹ Look at the headings of the rubric in the next table. You are going to answer the question "What level am I currently at?" In using this rubric and answering this question, begin by reviewing the criteria in the first column, Sub-Competencies. ▹ Next, think about yourself sitting in an interview. If you were asked to give an example of a time when you met or applied the criteria described in the Sub-Competencies column, what would your answer be? *Hint:* Your answer is the solid evidence you will use to determine the level you are currently at. For your solid evidence, you may rely on the anecdotes you listed in the Pre-Class Work. (You will always be provided with an example of the solid evidence on which you should rely.)

Rubric: Reflective Practice

Sub-Competencies of Ownership/ Self-Directedness	Novice Learner (Level 1)	Intermediate Learner (Level 2)	Competent Learner (Level 3)	Exceptional Learner (Level 4)
4. Reflects and Applies Lessons Learned Uses reflective practice to reflect on performance, to contemplate lessons learned, and to identify how to apply lessons learned to improve in the future, and then applies those lessons	RARELY uses reflective practice to reflect on performance, to contemplate lessons learned, and to identify how to apply lessons learned to improve in the future, and then applies those lessons.	SOMETIMES uses reflective practice to reflect on performance, to contemplate lessons learned, and to identify how to apply lessons learned to improve in the future, and then applies those lessons.	OFTEN uses reflective practice to reflect on performance, to contemplate lessons learned, and to identify how to apply lessons learned to improve in the future, and then applies those lessons.	CONSISTENTLY uses reflective practice to reflect on performance, to contemplate lessons learned, and to identify how to apply lessons learned to improve in the future, and then applies those lessons.

Step 2

Explain

Next, think about yourself talking with an attorney at a networking event. If you were asked to give an example of a time when you used certain criteria in the Sub-Competencies column, what would your answer be?

If you were asked to provide an example of a time when you faced an obstacle, and you were asked to describe how it worked out, you would likely respond by using reflective practice. For example, you could refer to one of your top skills/competencies and an anecdote from your Pre-Class Work.

To provide a response using the *Reflective Practice* rubric, it would be helpful to follow this outline:

- **What?** ("Provide an example of a time when you faced an obstacle.")
- **So what?** ("How did it work out?"—You made an adjustment to overcome that obstacle. What did you *do* that made a difference?)
- **Now what?** (How can you articulate what you did to show improvement *and* make the example relevant to your interviewer and the legal job for which you are applying?)

Step 3

Appraise

Now, suppose you are in an informational interview. What would your interviewer think about your answer? (Again, your answer is your "reflective practice." Generally, your answers to interview and networking questions should follow the structure: What? So what? Now what?)

Move horizontally across the rubric to decide on your answer and circle your choice. In other words, what level would your interviewer circle?

Remember that, in conducting a self-assessment, as you are doing here, you must *always* rely on solid, objective evidence that legal employers and attorneys would value to support your decision/conclusion.

Novice Learner (Level 1) **INTERMEDIATE LEARNER (LEVEL 2)** Competent Learner (Level 3) Exceptional Learner (Level 4)	Step **4**	**Assess** Finally, list the solid evidence you relied upon, or your plan for obtaining that evidence (diagnosing your learning need), in the space provided. In other words, what was the substance of the answer you gave during your "interview"? **Example Response** I circled Intermediate Learner. I am relying on the following solid evidence for *initiative/drive/strong work ethic.* I take initiative to overcome obstacles. When I owned my ice cream store, one morning my delivery driver left me a message stating that she could not make the delivery scheduled for later that day. It was a lot of ice cream and it was for an event, and so I decided that had to make that delivery myself. I called the driver and asked her for the names and numbers of people I could call about borrowing a refrigerated delivery truck and equipment. I also found coverage for the store while I was gone making the delivery. I wanted to make the delivery because the event needed to proceed flawlessly. I pulled it off—the event went well, and I went back to the store to finish the evening shift. I would apply this same initiative and drive in working with you and your firm. I am bound to face obstacles. I have the drive and solid work ethic to problem-solve and overcome them. I also learned from this experience: I started calling and confirming all scheduled deliveries at 3 PM the day before, and I made it incumbent upon the vendor to find an alternate, if necessary.*

* Whatever you write here should be in line with the level you circled in the table. This example provides the entire anecdote that the student relied upon to determine their level. However, you may abbreviate your answer by focusing on the details that are most relevant.

Note: Your plan for obtaining solid evidence (if you do not currently have it) may include some of the following options:

- Speaking with your favorite professor for suggestions and recommendations.
- Making an appointment with the career office.
- Speaking with your classmates, especially upper-division students.

Now it's your turn:

- Follow the steps described above to choose and define your current level of development in this area.
- List your solid evidence or your plan for obtaining that evidence.

Using Reflective Practice: Top Competencies/Skills

<table>
<tr><td>Steps
1
&
2</td><td>Reflect & Explain
What? The "what" is always the subject of the reflective practice for the week. For this assignment students have to reflect on their top competencies and skills. This is akin to being in an interview and answering the first part of the question "Provide an example of a time when…." (Here, it is using a competency or skill.)
So what? What is the anecdote you will use to answer the question, including describing the lesson(s) learned?
Now what? What adjustments will you make next time? And how can you put this part of your answer into context for legal employers and attorneys?</td></tr>
</table>

<table>
<tr><td rowspan="4">Steps
3
&
4</td><td>Novice Learner</td><td rowspan="4">Appraise & Assess
Circle your current level of development and then provide solid evidence for your selection.</td></tr>
<tr><td>Intermediate Learner</td></tr>
<tr><td>Competent Learner</td></tr>
<tr><td>Exceptional Learner</td></tr>
</table>

Pre-Class Work

1. Aligning Your Interests to Your Professional Identity

Now that you know the necessary critical skills and your top critical skills as they relate to professional identity formation, it is time for you to take the next step on your professional identity journey: aligning your interests to your professional identity.

Why do your interests matter? Because we know that "[t]here are only two good reasons psychologically for choosing your work or any other behavior: 1) you either inherently *enjoy the process* of doing that work, or 2) the work *supports your fundamental values*."[2]

"Enjoying the process" of doing your work is comparable to utilizing your interests—that is, being interested in and therefore liking the work that you do. In this chapter you are going to focus on your motivating interests, while in Chapter 4, you are going to focus on your values.

There is another important piece to focusing on your interests, however, and that is wellness.

2. Your Interests and Wellness

One way for you to take charge of your own future, practice wellness, and avoid falling into the massive statistic of depressed or substance-abusing attorneys is to identify, use, and match your skills, interests, and values while in law school and in the practice of law.

Bloomberg Law recently published an article titled *ANALYSIS: Well-Being in Law School—Law Students Aren't OK.*[3] The article noted that "[m]ost law students are struggling with mental health issues,... [and that] [o]ver 75% reported increased anxiety because of law school-related issues; over 50% reported experiencing depression.... A majority reported experiencing anxiety (77%), disrupted sleep (71%), and depression (51%)."

In addition, attorney and author Jordan Furlong urges law schools and bar admission programs to "warn aspiring lawyers about the poisonous culture of the profes-

---

2. Lawrence S. Krieger, The Hidden Stresses of Law School and Law Practice: Applying the New Science for a Fulfilling Life and Career 4 (emphasis in original).

3. Jessica R. Blaemire, *ANALYSIS: Well-Being in Law School—Law Students Aren't OK*, Bloomberg Law (Feb. 3, 2023, 5:00 AM EST). https://news.bloomberglaw.com/bloomberg-law-analysis/analysis-well-being-in-law-school-law-students-arent-ok.

sion they're entering."[4] He says that a focus on wellness should be "part of [a law student's] professional identity development." And while Mr. Furlong offers five steps that legal educators and regulators can take to help address this crisis, you too can directly address this crisis.

3. Taking Charge of Your Future

To directly address this crisis, you need to align your interests—which also help to make up part of your professional identity—with those of your future employer. This alignment, of using your interests on a daily basis, makes up one of the essential keys to choosing your work. In so doing, you are also choosing to practice wellness.

You have already identified your skill set in relation to the necessary critical lawyering skills. Now you will focus on identifying your interests as they relate to the necessary critical skills.

4. Exercise: Personal Interests

	List three examples of work/service/study experiences that occurred before or during law school in which something you did gave you positive meaning and energy.
1.	
2.	
3.	

4. *Send in Another Victim of Industrial Disease*, Jordan Furlong (Apr. 11, 2023), https://jordanfurlong.substack.com/p/send-in-another-victim-of-industrial.

	Which *specific* skills did you utilize in those experiences that yielded positive meaning and energy? Draw from the skills listed in Chapter 1.
1.	
2.	
3.	

	Briefly describe three examples of past work/service/study experiences during which others (especially senior people) recognized your contribution and you felt particularly good about the recognition.
1.	
2.	
3.	

	Which *specific* skills did you utilize in those experiences that yielded positive meaning and energy? Draw from the skills listed in Chapter 1.
1.	
2.	
3.	

Pre-Class Work Complete

In-Class Activity

1. Class Discussion: Review of Chapter 2

- Measuring Learning Objectives (Self-Assessment): Questions and Comments
- Ownership of Continuous Professional Development: Using Reflective Practice with Competencies and Skills

2. Class Discussion: Personal Interest and Wellness as a Critical Skill

Specifically knowing your personal interests, and how those interests align with the necessary critical lawyering skills, is an important step in your professional identity-formation journey. Utilizing your interests in your future legal practice is also a wonderful way for you to practice wellness.

There are many ways to practice wellness, and you may already engage in several activities that promote wellness for you. Whether you enjoy exercising, cooking, laughing with friends, or spending a quiet day at home, you should do your best to maintain and regularly incorporate your current wellness practices into your schedule.

At the same time, however, as you continue to move from student to lawyer, you will need additional resources to bolster your wellness practice. Because this transition includes your professional identity, you will want to do your best to align the necessary critical skills and your interests with the lawyering work you do.

a. Your Interests Matter

> *"To be a good lawyer, one has to be a healthy lawyer. Sadly, our profession is falling short when it comes to well-being. [Two recent studies]... reveal that too many lawyers and law students experience chronic stress and high rates of depression and substance use."*[5]

b. Your Interests Also Matter to Legal Employers

Our focus so far has been on identifying and aligning your interests with the necessary critical skills because doing so is one way to ensure you are happy and fulfilled in your legal practice.

But there is another reason that your interests and their connection to the necessary critical skills are important: your interests matter to your future legal employers.

When you target practice areas you are interested in and speak to legal professionals with whom you share a genuine interest, your enthusiasm and passion will show ("initiative" and "commitment to professional development... toward excellence" are two critical skills which require enthusiasm). This provides a "huge benefit" in that "it will make an impression on the employers you are most interested in and help you get hired by them.... Ultimately, a good career match for you is also a good hiring decision for the employer."[6]

---

5. Nat'l Task Force on Lawyer Well-Being, *The Path to Lawyer Well-Being: Practical Recommendations for Positive Change* 39 (Aug. 14, 2017), https://lawyerwellbeing.net/wp-content/uploads/2017/11/Lawyer-Wellbeing-Report.pdf.

6. *See* KRIEGER, *supra* note 2, at 6.

3. Activity: Personal Interest and Wellness Exercise: Identify Interests via Job Descriptions

The following job descriptions, from different practice areas, are pulled from a legal job board.

These posts further demonstrate that legal employers know and understand the importance in finding "the right person for the right job." The best candidate will demonstrate and communicate a match to the skills and interests the employer wants.

In using skills and interests in job descriptions, legal employers are (at a minimum) signaling which candidates should apply. When lawyers are not a good fit for an organization, firm, etc., it is most often the result of a misalignment between skills and interests (and also values, which we will discuss in the next chapter).

Instructions:

- Find a partner and read through the following job descriptions, noting how each one references or includes skills and interests.
- Be mindful of the interests and skills described. After you read through each description, fill in the boxes that follow, listing the skills and interests you find in each job description.

Note: There may not be a bright line between a skill and an interest. Do your best to separate each into the rows that follow. However, one helpful way to approach a skill versus an interest is as follows:

- The "interests" column is unique to the student. As you read each job description, ask whether any of the employer's stated interests align with a student's interests?
- The "skills" column is unique to the employer. Which specific skill(s) does the employer want the applicant to demonstrate?

Job Description #1: Public Interest

Employer focuses on ensuring the rights of underrepresented families in this community through legal services. With approximately 50 employees, Employer provides free legal services in the downtown area. Employer is a dynamic, fun place to work. Employer fosters a work environment that is motivating, collaborative, and fun, with plenty of opportunities for professional growth. We are working toward becoming a race-conscious legal services practice.

Employer empowers people identified as mentally or developmentally disabled to live more independent, secure, and satisfying lives through the enforcement of their legal rights and the advancement of their social and economic well-being. Employer helps its clients resolve problems in the areas of mental health care and treatment, housing rights, financial benefits, and medical insurance coverage. Employer regularly conducts community outreach to local homeless shelters and mental health clinics.

Job Description: After completing a training program consisting of written materials and staff lectures, the Law Clerk will apprentice with an attorney. Under the attorney's supervision, the Law Clerk will be responsible for providing direct legal assistance and representation to clients in public benefits-related cases. The Law Clerk also will be involved in research and system-reform projects, community and client education and outreach activities, and conducting client intake.

Job Duties:

1. Written, telephone, and in-person correspondence
2. Legal research and writing
3. Client intake and interviewing
4. Legal drafting, including letters, forms, and hearing briefs
5. Potential for client representation in a legal hearing

Desired Qualifications:

1. Ability to identify, investigate, and resolve client problems
2. Ability to work with legal concepts and materials
3. Ability to analyze, write, and present ideas clearly and concisely
4. Ability to work independently and as part of a team
5. Strong commitment to civil rights and the rights of mental health consumers, individuals living with HIV or AIDS and other disabilities, and individuals from underserved communities
6. Ability to treat mental health consumers and individuals living with HIV or AIDS and/or other disabilities with dignity and respect
7. Connections to and experience working with diverse populations, including communities of color and people living with disabilities
8. Passion for social justice and race equity as well as a desire to provide assistance to underserved populations

Interests	Skills

Job Description #2: In-House

Main Business: We are the next generation of the retail store. We pride ourselves on delivering a new kind of buying experience, and our friendly Customer Experience Experts bring the best of the store directly to you. We offer same-day delivery for today's premiere mobile devices with additional help and setup. Best of all...it's free! Each year we grow; we currently reach a total of 51 locations, including the UK, with more expansion on the horizon. Needless to say, it's an ambitious undertaking which requires a spirit of winning together and a *strong growth mindset.**

We value people who choose kindness and who are obsessed with delivering amazing experiences. We are helping today's premier companies navigate the shift from brick-and-mortar stores to online commerce that delivers a first-rate experience to the experience-obsessed. We deliver speed, kindness, and an outstanding value. Working alongside our founder is an executive team from leading retail, technology, and design organizations such as Apple, Facebook, and Amazon.

Preferred Qualifications:

- Prior intern/extern experience in an in-house legal setting
- 1+ year full-time work experience prior to law school

Proposed Types of Projects for Externs:

- Review and organize various documents (contracts, leases, employee files).
- Research and analyze relevant legal issues (both foreign and domestic) related to employment law, contracts, privacy and data security, industry-specific regulatory and compliance issues, litigation, etc.
- Research and analyze jurisdictional shifts to support expansion, including state, municipal, and international laws.
- Participate in the ideation and drafting of policies, processes, and procedures for company compliance and best practices.
- Build and maintain relationships with internal team.

Geographic Preference: San Francisco, California; Denver, Colorado; RTP, North Carolina; or Austin, Texas.

Interests	Skills

* *Skills:* Growth Mindset

"Dr. Dweck's research points to the significant benefit in developing a growth mindset in relation to learning, overcoming obstacles, and integrating negative feedback. A growth mindset embraces these challenges as an opportunity to learn, grow, and improve; for the same obstacles, a fixed mindset sees an inherent flaw or lack of intelligence that leads to failure."[7]

"Given the importance of having law students assume responsibility for their own professional development early in their careers, Dr. Dweck's presentation of the differences between fixed and growth mindsets is foundational for helping students understand the value of learning from their mistakes in achieving success."[8]

Job Description #3: Family Law/Litigation

Description: Our family law firm is currently seeking a full-time or part-time Law Clerk to assist our attorneys by preparing discovery and assembling and organizing case materials. This position will provide an excellent opportunity for practical legal experience. If you are interested in joining our growing team, please submit your résumé and cover letter.

Responsibilities: Legal research and drafting legal memoranda; reading and summarizing deposition transcripts; preparing legal and other correspondence; communicating with potential clients; assisting attorneys as needed.

Requirements:

- J.D. completed or in progress
- Proficient in MS Office, including Outlook, Word, and Excel
- Excellent communication, problem solving, interpersonal, organizational, and administrative skills, with accuracy and meticulous attention to detail
- Ability to take initiative, work independently, and prioritize multiple tasks with minimal supervision
- Solid vocabulary, grammar, spelling, punctuation, and proofreading skills
- Strong commitment both to individual assignments and team projects
- Ability to manage tight deadlines and work well under pressure.

continued

7. See Thiadora A. Pina, *Expanding and Teaching Lawyer Cultural Competence*, presentation at NALP, PDI Conference, Washington D.C. (September 2022) (summarizing ideas from Carol S. Dweck's, *Mindset: The New Psychology of Success* (2006)).

8. R. Lisle Baker, *supra* note 1, at 226.

continued

Benefits: Compensation is competitive. Our firm has a friendly team environment, great office perks, and an excellent benefits package, including medical and dental insurance, 15 days of paid time off, and 9 paid holidays. This is a great place to be valued and grow professionally.

Interests	Skills

4. Class Discussion: Wellness and Utilizing Your Skills and Interests in Practice

- From the employer's perspective, including a discussion of growth mindset.
- Making it personal—from the student perspective.

4

Your Values and Your Professional Identity

LEARNING OUTCOMES

- ▹ Discuss the connection between social competence and professional identity.
- ▹ Identify your top values and describe their personal significance.
- ▹ Summarize the role of values in professional identity.
- ▹ Discuss why values matter in legal practice.
- ▹ Discuss the ways law school supports your professional identity formation.
- ▹ Explain how a growth mindset is connected to your professional identity.

Reflection: Part A

Learning Objectives Self-Assessment

- To complete the following self-assessment exercise, read through the table below. The table lists the learning objectives from the previous chapter.
- If you can satisfy the objective, place a checkmark in the box.
- If you do not understand the objective or if you have more questions about the objective, place a question mark in the box.

Note: You need solid evidence to support your choices. Here your solid evidence is the ability to accomplish the stated learning objective.

AT THIS POINT, YOU SHOULD BE ABLE TO:	
	Describe the self-directed competency of "reflective practice" and illustrate its relation to your professional identity.
	List your top interests
	Summarize why utilizing interests matters in professional identity formation.
	Demonstrate concrete examples of different ways law school supports finding and utilizing your interests.
	Identify some ways attorneys and legal employers flag the interests and skills they find necessary in future employees.
	Explain the term "growth mindset" and apply it to a personal anecdote.

Reflection: Part B

Self-Directedness and Using Reflective Practice: Top Interests

This is the *Reflective Practice* rubric introduced in the previous chapter. This time, however, you are reflecting on the personal interests you identified in Chapter 3. Here you will continue to demonstrate solid professional development by purposely engaging in and tracking your reflective practice for Chapter 3.

For *Steps 3 & 4* in the following table, think about these two things: (1) the interests you identified in your Chapter 3 Pre-Class Work, and (2) the anecdotes you relied upon in Chapter 3 Pre-Class Work. Be sure to pay particular attention to the solid evidence you relied on and the objective evidence of what others (especially senior people) recognized about your contributions.

Also, remember that you must *always* rely on objective evidence to support your level of development. In other words, to support your chosen level, you need to provide *solid evidence* that legal employers would value. If you do not have that solid evidence, you must then *describe your plan for obtaining that evidence* (i.e., diagnose your learning needs).

Using Reflective Practice: Top Interests

Refer back to Chapter 3 for complete instructions on how to complete this assignment. Abbreviated instructions are provided below.

<table>
<tr><td>Steps
1
&
2</td><td colspan="2">Reflect
Using the Reflective Practice rubric from Chapter 3, answer the question "What level am I currently at?"
&
Explain
▹ What? The "what" is always the subject of the reflective practice for the week. For this assignment, you will reflect on your top interests from Chapter 3.
▹ So what? What is the anecdote you will use to answer the preceding question, including describing the lesson(s) learned?
▹ Now what? What adjustments will you make next time? How can you put this part of your answer into context for legal employers and attorneys? Using "critical skill language" will help here.</td></tr>
<tr><td rowspan="4">Steps
3
&
4</td><td>Novice Learner</td><td rowspan="4">Appraise & Assess
Circle your current level of development and provide solid evidence for your selection.</td></tr>
<tr><td>Intermediate Learner</td></tr>
<tr><td>Competent Learner</td></tr>
<tr><td>Exceptional Learner</td></tr>
</table>

Pre-Class Work

1. Exercise: Social Competency in Practice: Social Competency: Part B

Instructions:

Recall the Social Competency Reading and Activity from Chapter 2. After completing your chosen Chapter 2 activity, complete the following Social Competency Exercise.

Social Competency Exercise

1. Identify your completed activity.
2. Why did you choose this activity?
3. What new or enhanced social understanding, insight, or perspectives did your chosen activity provide? In other words, what did you learn?

4. Describe how completing your activity helped add to the solid evidence of your social competency development? (Be specific, remembering that your skill development is a process and will continue to evolve over time.)

5. Discuss the three skills you identified in Part A of this Activity in Chapter 2.		
	Competency	How did you use and rely upon that skill in completing this activity?
1		
2		
3		

6. Refer back to the Cultural Competency Milestone in Chapter 2. Discuss how this assignment fits (or not) into the "State of Cultural Competence" you chose in your Social Competency Exercise: Part A assignment. Here you will describe your Part B activity as it applies to your personal experiences and also discuss the solid evidence you are relying upon in providing the description.
7. Incorporate what you learned from this activity and how you will use that knowledge to keep expanding your social competence. State the specific steps you will take to grow and:

The behavior(s) you will…

Stop Doing:

Do Less Frequently:

SOCIAL COMPETENCE REFLECTION CIRCLE

The competencies you will…

Do More Frequently:

Start Doing (Specifically):

Exercise: Values Boxes[1]

What matters to you, and why is it important? With this exercise, you are going to build on those questions and identify your core values.

- First, take a moment to think about the values in your life, both in and outside of work. Be honest with yourself. The significance of this exercise is in choosing what is important to you; it is not about what others think should be important to you or worrying about what others think. There are literally hundreds of different values, but the value boxes on the next few pages include some of the most common ones.
- Second, rank all the boxes on a scale (1 = Very Important to Me, 2 = Important to Me, 3 = Not Important to Me) and write these numbers in the boxes.
- There are also two blank boxes that are to be used as "free boxes." The free boxes can represent a word or value that you feel is important but is not represented. You can add a value in one or both of the free boxes.

Remember, there is no "right" and "wrong" (no "good" or "bad" values) in this activity. We can perhaps compare this to our taste in pizza or movies. If you prefer ham and pineapple and your friend prefers pepperoni and mushroom, that does not mean your friend's taste in pizza is right and yours is wrong. It simply means that the two of you have different tastes.

- Third, cross out the Not Important to Me boxes and review the Very Important to Me and Important to Me boxes.
- Next, cross out the Important to Me boxes, and choose your *top five* core values from among the Very Important to Me boxes.

The remaining values you are left with should answer questions such as "What do I need to wake up happy and engaged?" and "How am I happy with myself?" Your top five values do not need to be ranked—you just need to select them.

- List your top five values in the chart after the values boxes exercise.

"Happiness is that state of consciousness which proceeds from the achievement of one's values."[2]

1. Adapted from Externships at UCI Law, 2018 (Director: D'Lorah Hughes).
2. Rand, Ayn. *The Virtue of Selfishness: A New Concept of Egoism*. New York: New American Library, 1961, p. 21.

1 Very Important to Me	2 Important to Me	3 Not Important to Me
SECURITY	COMPASSION	KINDNESS
FREEDOM	DEDICATION	DEPENDABILITY
ADVANCEMENT	LOYALTY	PEACE
WEALTH	MORALITY	EMPATHY
CREATIVITY	ACCOUNTABILITY	INDEPENDENCE
WORK	RELIGION	DIVERSITY
HUMOR	COOPERATION	COMPETITION
TRUSTWORTHINESS	RESPONSIBILITY	NON-CONFORMITY
PERFECTION	BALANCE	FAITH

1 Very Important to Me	**2** Important to Me	**3** Not Important to Me
LOVE	RECOGNITION	LEISURE
INTELLIGENCE	PROFESSIONALISM	ACCEPTANCE
FRIENDSHIP	PATIENCE	ADVENTURE
SPIRITUALITY	SUCCESS	FAMILY
COURAGE	POWER	BEAUTY
RESPECT	HONESTY	WISDOM
SPONTANEITY	INTEGRITY	HELPFULNESS
JUSTICE	HEALTH	KNOWLEDGE
TRADITION	BLANK BOX:	BLANK BOX:

Your Top Five Values	
1	
2	
3	
4	
5	

Provide anecdotes for each of your top five values. Describe why these five values rose to the top.

1	
2	

3	
4	
5	

Pre-Class Work Complete

In-Class Activity

1. Class Discussion: Review of Class 3

- Measuring Learning Objectives (Self-Assessment): Questions and Comments
- Ownership of Continuous Professional Development: Using Reflective Practice with Motivating Interests

2. Class Discussion: Analyze Social Competency Assignment

- A class discussion on your Social Competency assignment, with a particular emphasis on your completed Reflection Exercise.

3. Class Discussion: Describe Selection of Top Personal Values

- Discuss how personal values (such as religious or family values) that are not normally associated with professions affect choices related to practice and professional identity.

4. Class Discussion: Values and Professional Identity

In his article *Designing a Positive Psychology Course for Lawyers*, R. Lisle Baker writes that "[e]fforts to teach people to think like lawyers can unmoor students from their own values while serving as instruments of their clients."[2]

This begs the following questions: What role do values have in the traditional law school curriculum? When considering legal employment or when working with clients, what is the role of values in fostering professional identity formation?

You will recognize that several of the critical skills you are studying have a values component to them, directly or otherwise. For example, "commitment to firm/company/department and its goals and values," has a direct value component, while "initiative/drive/strong work ethic" requires a "values alignment" wherein your passion and engagement are difficult to maintain if your values are not aligned with the work you are doing.

5. Activity: Values in the Legal Profession

Recall from Chapter 2 that "[t]here are only two good reasons psychologically for choosing your work or any other behavior: 1) you either inherently *enjoy the process* of doing that work, or 2) the work *supports your fundamental values*."[3]

Having already identified your top values, you will now explore the ways in which legal employers are also interested in values. Remember that "a good career match for you is also a good hiring decision for the employer,"[4] and this includes aligning your values.

---

2. R. Lisle Baker, *Designing a Positive Psychology Course for Lawyers*, 51 Suffolk U. L. Rev. 207, 235 (2018), https://ssrn.com/abstract=3271713. Thiadora Pina is indebted to R. Lisle Baker for providing this paper.

3. Lawrence S. Krieger, The Hidden Stresses of Law School and Law Practice: Applying the New Science for a Fulfilling Life and Career 4 (emphasis in original).

4. *Id.* at 6.

Instructions:

- Using the tables that follow, review the job descriptions in Chapter 3. Identify three values the legal employers signaled were important. Write those values down in the first box below.
- After writing down those values, use the next text box to briefly describe the solid evidence a student might rely upon to demonstrate their possession of each of those values.

Job Description #1 Employer's Values	Solid Evidence—Examples of Student Demonstrating Those Values
	1.
	2.
	3.
Job Description #2 Employer's Values	**Solid Evidence—Examples of Student Demonstrating Those Values**
	1.
	2.
	3.
Job Description #3 Employer's Values	**Solid Evidence—Examples of Student Demonstrating Those Values**
	1.
	2.
	3

6. Role Play and Scenario: Moving Values Theory into Practice

Insurance, Immigration, and Values

Instructions:
We've been discussing values in the following contexts:

1. Identifying your values.
2. Understanding your employer's and their clients' values.
3. The benefits and burdens of aligning your values with those of your employer and their clients.

Within this context, here is a true story. Read through the scenario and answer the questions that follow.

David, a second-year associate at a mid-sized firm, just got back to his office. He was skipping along the way because he was so excited. "I am finally going to conduct my first EUO—woohoo!"

An EUO is an *examination under oath*—similar to a deposition, except that no lawsuit has been filed. Under the terms of most commercial and personal insurance policies, the insurer has the right (an insurance policy is a contract, after all) to request an EUO (or "call an EUO") as part of its investigation when a claim is filed. In calling the EUO, the insurer refers the claim to legal counsel (in this case, David), who then issues the demand that the insured/claimant present for an EUO. An insurer has the right to deny the claim if the insured fails to attend the EUO.

David is ready. He's been in charge of this file ever since a managing partner, his litigation manager Indira, dropped the newly opened file on his desk seven weeks ago. It was the first file assigned to David for which he was lead counsel. The claimant was Robert Perry. Mr. Perry filed a claim because several of his work vans were badly vandalized. Mr. Perry parked his work vans at a remote location rather than at his office. His office was located downtown, where parking was limited and expensive.

When David first received the file, he and Indira discussed the claim. Because Mr. Perry's vans were customized, contained expensive equipment and tools, and there was a "loss of use" provision in the policy, the claim was worth thousands and thousands of dollars. "It's a big payout, David," Indira said. "Let's see what we can do." So, David combed through the file, made phone calls, visited the site of the vandalism, and researched the relevant policy provisions.

David also looked into Mr. Perry's background and business to make sure that Perry didn't have any reason to vandalize his own vans. As David kept digging, he found it odd that he had trouble finding out about Mr. Perry's background. David thought to himself, "Perry is running a successful business. He couldn't have started this business out of thin air." David kept investigating and working the file, along with the other dozens of files that were assigned to him.

Weeks later, David felt confident that his investigation was complete. He recently received notice from the Social Security Administration, one of the agencies he had contacted to learn more about Mr. Perry's background. He spoke with Indira and she agreed—it was time to call the EUO.

Because this was David's first EUO, Indira planned to sit in with him, which made David a little nervous. "What if I ask the wrong questions, not enough questions, too many questions—ahhh!" He shook his head. "It's going to be fine," he thought to himself. "I ran just about everything past Indira. She wouldn't have given me this chance unless she knew I was ready. I'm ready!"

The EUO was scheduled for early the next day. David arrived at the office really early; he couldn't sleep anyway. He was at his desk and buried in the file when he heard a knock on his office door. He looked up. It was Indira. "Show time!" she said. "What? Wait? What time is . . ." before David finished his sentence, Indira started down the hall. "Show time!" she shouted back over her shoulder.

David put all his papers back in order and headed to the conference room. The court reporter was set up at the end of the conference table. David sat next to Indira, organized his papers, and then nodded to his assistant as a signal to bring in the insured. A few moments later, the insured Robert Perry walked through the door. Mr. Perry was wearing a blue blazer, a white button-down shirt, and khakis. Mr. Perry had a few wisps of gray in an otherwise full head of hair. David noticed Mr. Perry's hair because David was starting to see some thinning hair on the crown of his own head. "Great hair!" David thought to himself.

David stood and greeted Mr. Perry. Mr. Perry sat down across the conference room table from David. David formally introduced himself, noted they were "on the record," and the EUO began.

All was going well. "He's doing a great job; he came prepared," Indira thought to herself. Then, David reached for one of the papers on the table Indira had been looking at. Indira gave David a quick nod, and David then showed the paper to Mr. Perry.

"Mr. Perry," David said, "This document was issued by the Social Security Administration. According to the Social Security Administration, the social security number you listed on your application for insurance was issued to a gentleman named Yung Xi, in Hawaii, in 1937. Now Mr. Perry, I'm having trouble understanding this paper. Can you help me?"

Mr. Perry suddenly looked sick—physically sick. David quickly looked back down at the paper. Mr. Perry's physical appearance was a little upsetting to David. David kept looking at the paper. "Well, you certainly don't look like you were born in 1937, and you told me, under oath, that your name is Robert Perry. Are you sure you can't help me because I'm really confused."

Mr. Perry shook his head no. "I can't help. I don't understand why they would say that."

"Are you sure?" David asked.

Mr. Perry looked down and then away, "I don't know."

"Okay," David said, "I just have a few more questions."

David finished his last question about ten minutes later. He then stood up, and Mr. Perry followed. David shook Mr. Perry's hand and thanked him for coming. "The insurer will be in touch shortly regarding your claim," David said. Mr. Perry simply nodded as he quickly and quietly left the room.

David was happy with how his first EUO went. And it ended up that David was pleased to have met Mr. Perry. Mr. Perry reminded David of his own family. David was a second-generation American whose family worked really hard to get to America. David's grandparents always told him stories about coming to the United States, and David had visited his grandparents' home country many times. David's family was so proud of him, and he of them.

David looked over at Indira who said, "Good work. That's a quick denial and onto the next file. Let the insurer know you confirmed the fake social security number. For your next . . ."

"Wait," David said. "Wait." David sat back down and rubbed his forehead. "Mr. Perry paid insurance premiums for over ten years. He never missed a payment, and he was never late. He's paid thousands of dollars to the insurance company. This is his first claim, and . . ."

Indira stopped David with a wave of her hand, "And?" she asked. Mr. Perry's sick look flashed in David's mind. At that moment, David felt he probably looked exactly the same. Indira left the room.

Later that day, David finished the report to the insurer—misrepresentation in the application for insurance voided the policy. The misrepresentation did not need to be material. In this case, although Mr. Perry's use of a fake social security number was not material to the claim, it was a misrepresentation, which meant that the insurance policy could be void. The insurer didn't have to, and wasn't going to, pay Mr. Perry a dime—claim denied. David finished the report and went home for the day.

The next day, David got a call from the insurer, his client. "Congratulations! Job well done!" It was tough for David to hold onto the phone. This didn't feel good. Then David's client asked, "Should we call ICE and report the fake social security number? What's our next move?"

David suddenly felt sick again. "Next move?" David asked, "What next move? The claim is denied. You're happy and we'll never hear from Mr. Perry again. Let it go—just let it go!"

"What? Alright, Davey. Take it easy. Geez," said the insurer.

"Sorry," David said, lowering his tone. "I had a rough night. It wasn't your fault, and I shouldn't have raised my voice. Thanks so much for calling. I appreciate it. But let's just let this one end here, okay? I'm sure we'll never hear from Mr. Perry again. I'm always happy to work with you, and I look forward to helping with the next claim."

After a long pause, the insurer said, "Well, okay then. Indira is a great lawyer, and I know she only hires the best. You did a great job tracking down that fake number! I'm sure we'll be back in touch soon."

David got along with Indira and most of the people at the firm, but he never really liked the work or going to work. He thought a new firm and a change of scenery would help. After another year at the firm, he began looking for a new job. He never forgot Robert Perry. No one at the firm or insurance company ever heard from Robert Perry again.

Use the values boxes from the Pre-Class Work to answer the following questions:

1. Identify at least three of the firm's values.

1	
2	
3	

2. Identify at least three of Indira's values.

1	
2	
3	

3. Identify at least three of David's values.

1	
2	
3	

4. Identify the issue(s) regarding client service. Does it have anything to do with values?

____

____

____

____

____

____

____

5. The firm has a website. The website describes the firm's "core values" and its mission. Do you think the values listed on the website match the values you've identified? Why or why not—and be specific.

____

____

____

____

____

____

____

7. Class Discussion: Putting It All Together: Visualize Your Professional Identity and How Law School Can Help

Law school is the ideal time to focus on your professional identity, and you must take full advantage of the many ways law school can help build your professional identity.

Now that you have a solid understanding of your skills, interests, and values as they relate to the necessary critical skills and the practice of law, look at the next graphic. Here are some examples of how law school can help as you work and move from student to lawyer. Remember, however, that it is up to you to be proactive and involved.

The many offices at a law school are also partners in your professional journey. Career services, academic success, alumni relations, professors, etc.: all of these offices and people can connect you with ideas and opportunities, from panels to engaged alumni, from study habits to research opportunities. Your law school is your professional partner.

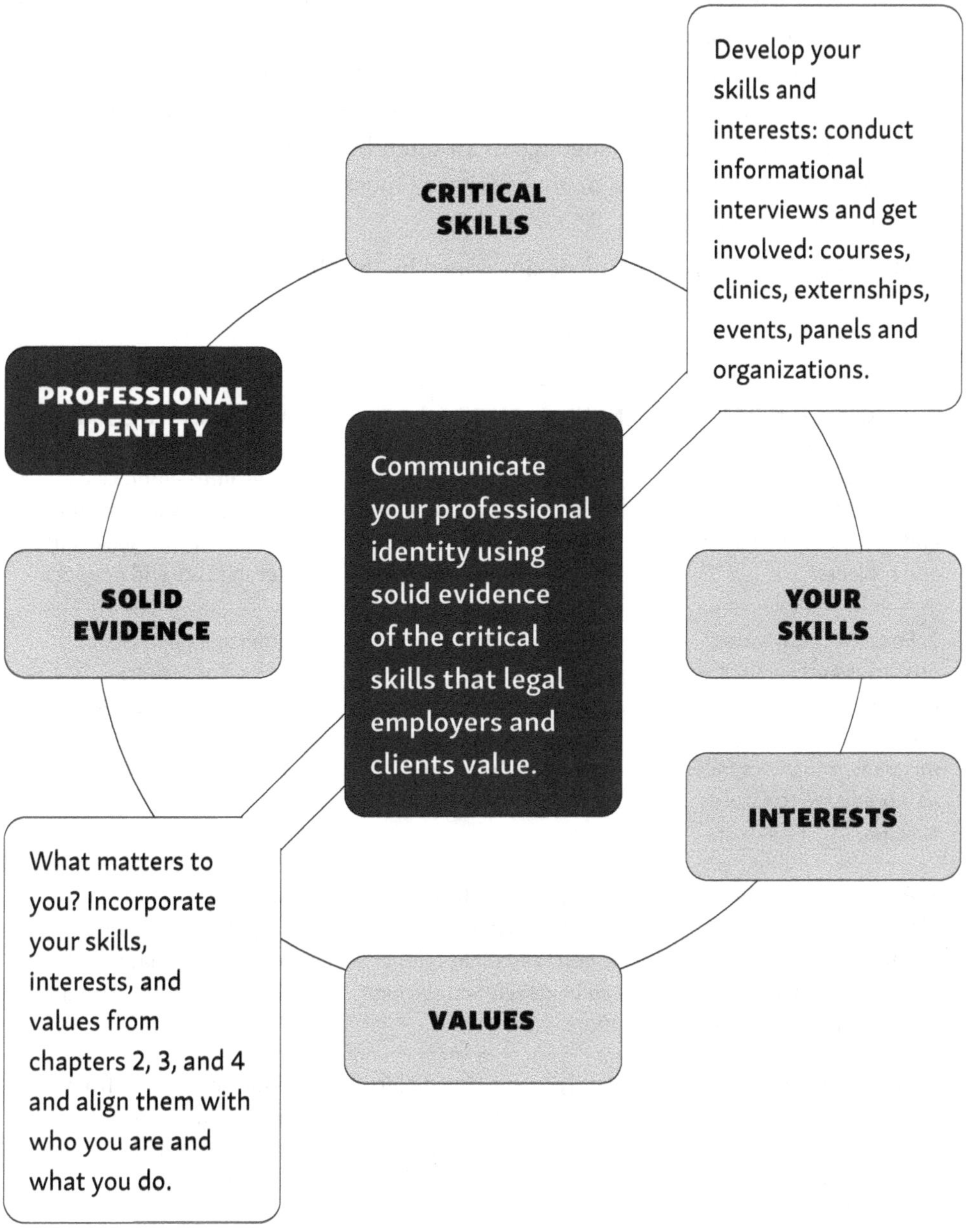

8. Growth Mindset and Professional Identity Formation

In the second job description above, you encountered the term "growth mindset." This skill is often emphasized and sought after, especially for new lawyers. When new lawyers present to the office, so much of the work they are tasked with completing is new. Afterall, it is often said that law school does not do a very good job at teaching law students how to actually practice law!

Given this work environment, having a growth mindset is key. Law students must see challenges as opportunities for learning, and they must respond well to criticism and use feedback constructively to improve their mastery and performance. These are two key points to having a growth mindset. And, given that learning to practice law is akin to learning a new language in an often high-stakes environment, there are bound to be many setbacks that new lawyers must embrace and see as opportunities to grow and learn.

Below is a *Growth Mindset* rubric developed by the Holloran Center.

Rubric: Growth Mindset Milestone[5]

SUB-COMPETENCIES	NOVICE LEARNER	INTERMEDIATE LEARNER
1. Embraces challenges as opportunities for learning and seeks out stretch tasks and projects.	**Rarely** embraces challenges as opportunities for learning and seeks out stretch tasks and projects.	**Sometimes** embraces challenges as opportunities for learning and seeks out stretch tasks and projects.
2. Effectively navigates obstacles and persists in the face of setbacks, is not discouraged by mistakes, and views failure as a predicate to future success.	**Rarely** persists in the face of setbacks, is not discouraged by mistakes, and views failure as a predicate to future success.	**Sometimes** persists in the face of setbacks, is not discouraged by mistakes, and views failure as a predicate to future success.
3. Puts forth full effort and views effort as a path to mastery and understands that talent can be developed through effort.	**Rarely** views effort as a path to mastery and understands that talent can be developed through effort.	**Sometimes** views effort as a path to mastery and understands that talent can be developed through effort.
4. Responds well to failure and feedback and learns from failure and criticism and uses feedback constructively.	**Rarely** learns from failure and criticism and uses feedback constructively.	**Sometimes** learns from failure and criticism and uses feedback constructively.
5. Finds lessons and inspiration in the successes of others.	**Rarely** finds lessons and inspiration in the successes of others.	**Sometimes** finds lessons and inspiration in the successes of others.

5. *Growth Mindset Competency Milestone*, Univ. of St. Thomas Sch. of Law, https://law.stthomas.edu/about/centers-institutes/holloran-center/competency-milestones/growth-mindset/index.html (last visited Sep. 10, 2024).

SUB-COMPETENCIES	COMPETENT LEARNER	EXCEPTIONAL LEARNER
1. Embraces challenges as opportunities for learning and seeks out stretch tasks and projects.	**Often** embraces challenges as opportunities for learning and seeks out stretch tasks and projects.	**Consistently** embraces challenges as opportunities for learning and seeks out stretch tasks and projects
2. Effectively navigates obstacles and persists in the face of setbacks, is not discouraged by mistakes, and views failure as a predicate to future success.	**Often** persists in the face of setbacks, is not discouraged by mistakes, and views failure as a predicate to future success.	**Consistently** persists in the face of setbacks, is not discouraged by mistakes, and views failure as a predicate to future success.
3. Puts forth full effort and views effort as a path to mastery and understands that talent can be developed through effort.	**Often** views effort as a path to mastery and understands that talent can be developed through effort.	**Consistently** views effort as a path to mastery and understands that talent can be developed through effort.
4. Responds well to failure and feedback and learns from failure and criticism and uses feedback constructively.	**Often** learns from failure and criticism and uses feedback constructively.	**Consistently** learns from failure and criticism and uses feedback constructively.
5. Finds lessons and inspiration in the successes of others.	**Often** finds lessons and inspiration in the successes of others.	**Consistently** finds lessons and inspiration in the successes of others.

Focus on the sub-competencies column to have a better understanding of what exactly a growth mindset requires. As you work your way through the rubric, understand and think of the solid evidence you will rely upon to determine your current level while also giving thought to what action steps you will take to progress to the next level and gain mastery of this skill.

Instructions:

- Write out an anecdote on the following page that demonstrates your solid evidence for one of the sub-competencies listed in the *Growth Mindset* rubric.

9. In-Class Scenario: Your Professional Identity in Practice: Growth Mindset and Professional Development Early in Your Legal Career

Scenario: Violet

Instructions:

Analyze and help Violet with her first-year lawyering professional development. Read through the scenario and answer all questions at the end.

Note: This scenario is a typical of a lawyer's six-month or year-end review process. Managers often ask lawyers to come up with goals and plans that the lawyer will implement before the next process review takes place. In effect, it will be your responsibility to take charge of your professional identity.

Violet has just finished her first ten months at a small but growing tech company, SmartRing! So far, the company has one product on the market—a tiny, finger-sized version of a smart watch.

While Violet was in law school, all she wanted to do was work for a technology company. Wait—that's not entirely true. The truth is that she was not exactly sure what she wanted to do.

But her family, especially her parents, told her (over and over) that if she went to law school, she would be crazy to not end up working at a technology firm. Her family felt that technology is where the money and security are.

When Violet was job hunting, she could hear the voices of her parents in her head: "You have student loans to pay, and the non-profit work you did before law school won't begin to cover those loans. Get a corporate job!"

So, Violet accepted the job that SmartRing! offered her. SmartRing! was the only tech company that made her an offer. Because Violet felt she should work in tech (and she didn't have other high-paying offers), she didn't feel that she could ask many questions during her interviews about the company, the legal department, or the job.

Violet's three best law school pals seem so happy. They followed their hearts and are working at their dream jobs (one at the public defender's office, one at a trusts/estates firm, and the other at a non-profit organization). Although Violet is making more money than any of them, she finds herself a little lost and more than a little low at the end of each day. But she knows that she wants to continue working at SmartRing! The team of people there is awesome. She just needs to find something in her job that connects better with what she cares about.

Violet now knows that most corporate law departments have sub-departments that report to the general counsel or chief legal officer (CLO), the lead attorney for the company. Violet was hired to do "transactional" work (negotiating contracts) and to help with a big intellectual property project. She isn't at all interested in the projects on her desk, but she works hard and does really good work.

Every other week, the whole twenty-person legal department has a staff meeting. People dial in from their remote locations or join together in the headquarters conference room. The lead of each legal department area (sub-department) gives an update on their respective area during that meeting. Violet now knows that the sub-department leads address certain topics (intellectual property, human resources, corporate law, commercial transactions, ethics and compliance, operations, litigation, etc.).

At the last couple of these staff meetings, the head of the compliance team has been talking about a big "values" project. He is working with the human resources department and with small virtual teams around the company to help define a new set of values for the company. For the first time, Violet hears something that really resonates with her! After the meeting, she sits in her cube thinking about what it would be like to work on such an interesting project. But she is the newest attorney at SmartRing! and so the lowest on the totem pole. Violet wouldn't want to rock the boat or cause any issues among the attorneys by asking to work on anything different than what she is currently doing.

Then, today, Violet received an automated email from the CEO and head of HR alerting her (and the rest of the company) to the annual performance review process. She has never heard of anything like this, and she hunkers down in her cube to figure out what's required of her.

The email says that Violet has two weeks to fill out three online forms. After that, she will have a formal meeting with the CLO and the two attorneys for whom she does work—the head transactional attorney and the head intellectual property (IP) attorney.

Part I

It looks like Part 1 of the review process is an online chart that shows how Violet's own job actually helps the company meet its strategic goals. The company's strategic goals are focused on great customer service, reaching $1B in sales next year, and becoming number one in the marketplace in smart rings. Violet is pretty creative, and she thinks she can easily accomplish this first task. After all, she does work with customers and internal departments, and her IP project is probably indirectly helping the company differentiate its products. Check!

Part 2

For the second part of this review process, Violet needs to list her own quarterly goals for the next fiscal year. Because she recently had a conversation with the lead transactional attorney to talk about goals, Violet feels that she can also complete this within two weeks if she has your help. Can you help Violet by defining three different goals for her?

1	
2	
3	

Part 3

The third and final part of the review process is a professional development plan. Violet gets a sickening feeling in her stomach when she realizes that she is in charge of coming up with what she would like to do for her own professional development. *And worse... maybe she will always be in charge of deciding that?* A required professional identity class comes briefly to her mind.

In Violet's legal team staff meetings, she has heard that some legal department employees go to networking events and seminars. Violet had never realized that maybe those events were part of "professional development," but this gets her thinking.

Violet needs to identify three or four proposals for her own professional development for next year. She will need to pitch these ideas to the CLO. Can you help her with this project? No pressure... but please recognize that doing this well could be the key to Violet's happiness.

Be creative, and make sure to include a reason that these ideas might be beneficial to the department and/or the company, and to Violet personally. Violet senses that the last thing the CLO will want to do is invest a lot of money in her and then have her take her newfound talents to another company.

Be clear, concise, and ready to answer questions.

Professional Development Plan for Violet

1	Proposed professional development: How might this benefit SmartRing!?
2	Proposed professional development: How might this benefit SmartRing!?
3	Proposed professional development: How might this benefit SmartRing!?

Part 4

Similar to Job Description #2 in Chapter 3, Violet's CLO is also obsessed with growth-mindset theory. It is a common thread that runs through the CLO and Violet's team.

So, as part of her development plan, the CLO also asked Violet to connect her proposed professional development ideas to the *Growth Mindset* rubric above. The CLO wants to see solid evidence of Violet's growth mindset improving over time.

1	Growth Mindset Sub-Competency: How is solid evidence demonstrated?
2	Growth Mindset Sub-Competency: How is solid evidence demonstrated?

10. Class Discussion: In-Class Scenario: Your Professional Identity in Practice—Violet and SmartRing!

- Discuss the role of networking and building relationships while at work.
- Discuss the role of a growth mindset at work.

5

Application of Skills to Practice

Building Relationships and Networking

LEARNING OUTCOMES

- Describe the process for, benefits of, and link between networking and business development.
- Analyze and measure your progress/benchmarks in developing a networking plan.
- Define the STAR method and develop, choose, and communicate appropriate STAR method examples.
- Explain and apply active listening skills to oral communication.

Reflection: Part A

Learning Objectives Self-Assessment

- To complete the following self-assessment exercise, read through the table below. The table lists the learning objectives from the previous chapter.
- If you can satisfy the objective, place a check mark in the box.
- If you do not understand the objective or if you have more questions about the objective, place a question mark in the box.

Note: You need solid evidence to support your choices. Here, your solid evidence is the ability to accomplish the stated learning objective.

AT THIS POINT, YOU SHOULD BE ABLE TO:	
	Discuss the connection between social competence and professional identity.
	List your top values and describe their personal significance.
	Summarize the role of values in professional identity.
	Discuss why values matter in legal practice.

Reflection: Part B

Self-Directedness and Using Reflective Practice: Top Values

This section refers to the *Reflective Practice* rubric introduced in Chapter 3. This time, however, you are reflecting on the top values you identified in Chapter 4. Here, you will continue to demonstrate solid professional development by purposely engaging in and tracking your reflective practice for Chapter 4.

For *Steps 3 & 4* in the following table, think about these two things: (1) the values you identified in your Chapter 4 Pre-Class Work and (2) the anecdotes you relied upon in your Chapter 4 Pre-Class Work.

Also, remember that you must *always* rely on objective evidence to support your level of development. In other words, to support your chosen level, you need to have *solid evidence* that legal employers would value. If you do not have that solid evidence, you must then *describe your plan for obtaining that evidence* (which demonstrates problem solving).

Using Reflective Practice: Top Values

Refer back to Chapter 3 for complete instructions on how to complete this assignment. Abbreviated instructions are provided below.

<table>
<tr><td>Steps
1
&
2</td><td>Reflect
Using the Reflective Practice rubric from Chapter 3, answer the question "What level am I currently at?"
&
Explain
• What? The "what" is always the subject of the reflective practice for the week. For this assignment, you will reflect on your top values from Chapter 4.
• So what? What is the anecdote you will use to answer the preceding question, including describing the lesson(s) learned?
• Now what? What adjustments will you make next time? How can you put this part of your answer into context for legal employers and attorneys? Using "critical skill language" will help here.</td></tr>
</table>

<table>
<tr><td rowspan="4">Steps
3
&
4</td><td>Novice Learner</td><td rowspan="4">Appraise & Assess
Circle your current level of development and then provide solid evidence for your selection.</td></tr>
<tr><td>Intermediate Learner</td></tr>
<tr><td>Competent Learner</td></tr>
<tr><td>Exceptional Learner</td></tr>
</table>

Pre-Class Work

1. Networking and Business Development[1]

Networking and business development are closely related critical skills that you must develop and demonstrate in law school and early in your career. Both skills are crucial to legal practice.

First, all legal employers prioritize networking and building professional connections, though the specific skills emphasized in these areas may vary by practice area and employer. The key here is that you must determine which networking skills apply to the employer and practice area that interests you the most.

This is information you want to fully understand *before* you commit to any particular practice area. For example, if networking to find, retain and build a strong client base is not something that you at all want to do—i.e., build a book of business—then you do not want to choose the law firms and/or practice areas that require this. Again, the key here is that you must determine which networking skills apply to which employers and practice areas as you build your professional identity.

a. Putting Networking to Work for You

Do not be discouraged by this. One of the great aspects of the legal profession is its diversity, offering numerous areas of law and various ways to practice. You will find the area and type of practice that is the best match to your skills, interests, and values. The only caveat here is this: you must be intentional in this choice.

For example, some legal employers and practice areas place particular emphasis on forming professional networks; building and maintaining relationships; being involved in industry, civic, and professional groups; understanding the client and its business; building a referral network; or being able to initiate face-to-face meetings with contacts. You are able to decide which of these networking roles suits you best.

By acquiring these skills early, students can demonstrate their professional development to prospective employers because they will already be operating at the level the employer expects from a new lawyer.

Thus, while in law school, you should have two networking goals: (1) to gain experience in your most promising employment areas that will give you enough information to eliminate or confirm your options, and (2) to gain enough solid evidence to demonstrate this skill.

Legal employers are increasingly looking for new lawyers who are capable of creating relationships with clients and other legal stakeholders. From the very begin-

1. See generally Neil W. Hamilton, Roadmap: The Law Student's Guide to Meaningful Employment 143 (2023).

ning, legal employers are interested in those law students who have developed a strong network of professional contacts and networks, and it is easy to understand why: this is a transferable skill. If you can do it in law school, you likely can transfer that skill and knowledge to the office.

2. Networking and Business Development as Critical Skills

Remember the critical lawyering skills listed in Chapter 1. In reviewing that list, it is easy to see the crucial importance of developing your networking and business development skills.

- Integrity/honesty/trustworthiness, including building relationships
- Initiates and maintains strong team and work relationships
- Commitment to firm/department/company and its goals and values
- Dedication to client service/understanding of and responsiveness to client, including listening

The list of critical skills that have a networking and business development component to them is quite long.

As you can see, developing this skill is certainly important to your professional identity: Which practice area will you choose? Which professional relationships will you develop? What type of clients/business/industry will you work with? Who will support your professional journey; and in turn, whose professional journey will you support? The answers to all of these questions are rooted in your in networking and business development skills.

3. Exercise: Networking Skills Assessment[2]

> The following self-assessment will help you focus on your networking and business development skills. It will allow you to see where you currently are, what to focus on, and ways you can continue to build this skill so that you may demonstrate it with solid evidence.

1. How much time do you spend networking each week?

___

2. Adapted from Neil Hamilton, *Assessment of Developmental Stage of Networking Skills for Section III, Chapter K* (2017), https://www.americanbar.org/groups/departments_offices/publishing/books/roadmap/.

2. Have you set clear networking goals?

YES	NO

Answer the following questions using this scale:

1	2	3	4	5
NOT AT ALL	A LITTLE	SOME	SUBSTANTIALLY	COMPLETELY

3. Have you identified the various types of relationships that will be necessary to help you confirm or eliminate your most promising employment options?

4. What long-term relationships do you have that will help you? Consider professors, mentors, employers, coaches, etc.

___

5. Have you identified the types of long-term relationships that will help you gain experience in the critical skills that you need to develop?

6. Have you identified groups or individuals with whom you would want to network (including the people you want to serve, i.e., future clients and the employers who represent these clients)?

7. Do you have at least two strong faculty references who know you well enough to provide a very strong reference regarding the specific skills you want to emphasize?

YES	NO

8. If yes, list them. If not, list potential faculty references.

___

9. Do you have at least one strong non-faculty reference from a senior person regarding specific skills you want to emphasize?

YES	NO

10. If yes, list that person. If not, list your plan/ideas for obtaining that non-faculty reference.

____

____

____

____

Instructions:

As you know, self-development and reflection contribute to your professional identity. Think about your networking goals and your plan for achieving those goals.

- Review the rubric below.
- Consider the solid evidence you possess that legal employers would value. Circle the level of development that best aligns with your solid evidence, and then discuss the solid evidence supporting your assessment. Remember, in conducting this or any self-assessment, you must always rely on solid, objective evidence to support your decision/conclusion.
- If you do not have that evidence, you must know and be able to describe your plan for obtaining that evidence (diagnose your learning needs).

Rubric: Law Student's Networking Skills Development

Student Level	Critical Skill Development: Professional Identity + Networking
Beginning Networker	• Student has yet to strategically identify experienced people in the student's most promising career options. • Student does not or rarely attends student organization or career services events/panels. • Student does not or rarely attends bar association and professional/civic/volunteer events. • Student does not or rarely engages in follow-up with contacts.
Moderate Networker *(continued)*	• Student is beginning to focus on experienced people in the student's most promising career options. • Student regularly attends student organization, bar association, and professional/civic/volunteer events and initiates conversations with presenters and attendees. • Student occasionally follows up with contacts. • Student occasionally initiates informational interviews with contacts.

Moderate Networker *(continued)*	• Student is well prepared for informational interview by engaging in research before the meeting, asking specific and relevant questions, not talking too much, and obtaining additional referrals. • Student inconsistently maintains relationships with contacts from informational interviews.
Strong Networker	• Student networks with experienced people in the student's most promising career options field. • Student has regular involvement in and helps student organizations, bar associations, and professional/civic/volunteer groups and is beginning to establish a strong, positive reputation within those groups. • Student regularly initiates conversations at these events and activities and usually follows up. • Student initiates and has had several informational interviews and is well prepared for those informational interviews, leaving a good impression. • Student is developing solid evidence of their networking and business development strengths that a legal employer would accept.
Expert Networker	• Student is strategically focused on networking with experienced people. • Student regularly attends and helps student organizations, bar association sections, and professional/civic/volunteer groups and has established a strong, positive relationship among them. • Student initiates meaningful conversations with professionals at these events and regularly follows up. • Student seeks out informational interviews with contacts in areas of interest, is well prepared and professional during the meetings, looks for ways to benefit contacts, obtains referrals and helps other students or those in the field, follows through with information gained from the meetings, and maintains regular relationships with professionals. • Student has strong evidence of networking and business development skills that legal employers value.

Beginning Networker	**Moderate Networker**
Strong Networker	**Expert Networker**

The solid evidence for my selection, or my plan for obtaining it is:

____

____

____

____

____

Answer the following questions using this scale:

1	2	3	4	5
NOT AT ALL	A LITTLE	SOME	SUBSTANTIALLY	COMPLETELY

11. Do you have a clear timetable to assess whether you are succeeding in your networking plan with respect to the following areas?
    a. Are you achieving your specific networking goals (e.g., having a monthly goal to conduct one informational interview on an area of employment)?
    b. Are your most promising employment options the best fit for you?
    c. Are you demonstrating to senior-level people sufficient evidence of specific skills that your potential employers will accept?
    d. Are you gaining experience through employment or volunteer opportunities in the specific skills you want to emphasize?
    e. Are you deepening existing relationships (e.g., meeting with a current connection once a month to discuss new topics)?
    f. Are you building new relationships (e.g., attending one networking event and finding at least two new contacts)?
12. Refer back to the rubric above and circle where you see yourself in terms of implementing your networking plan. You will want to revisit this plan periodically, and you may want to include it in your SMART Goals assignment in Chapter 6.

Beginning Networker	Moderate Networker
Strong Networker	Expert Networker

The solid evidence for my selection, or my plan for obtaining it is:

____

____

____

____

____

____

Answer the following questions using this scale:

1	2	3	4	5
NOT AT ALL	A LITTLE	SOME	SUBSTANTIALLY	COMPLETELY

13. Have you thought through how to ask a new contact for an informational interview? Or have you conducted informational interviews?
14. What types of questions will/did you ask in an informational interview? Possible examples include:
    (1) How did you get your start in this area of law?
    (2) How did you decide on this area of law?
    (3) What do you like about what you do?
    (4) What would you change about your work if you could?
    (5) What do you wish you knew when you started?
    (6) What do you think will change about this area of law in the next five to ten years?

Write at least three questions (different from the example questions) that you asked or would ask:

1	
2	
3	

15. Do you proactively seek feedback on your networking plan?
16. Do you reflect on the successes and failures that you are experiencing in networking?
17. Do you revisit and revise your networking plan as you gain experience?
18. Do you present solid evidence of networking experience to potential employers?

Pre-Class Work Complete

In-Class Activity

1. Class Discussion: Review of Class 4

- Measuring Learning Objectives (Self-Assessment): Questions and Comments
- Ownership of Continuous Professional Development: Using Reflective Practice with Values

2. Class Discussion: Networking Skills Assessment Exercise

Paying particular attention to the solid evidence you relied upon in completing this assignment, how is networking in law school adding to your professional identity?

3. Activity: Networking and Demonstrating Effective Oral Communication by Implementing the STAR Method[3]

Instructions:

- ▹ On the following pages are questions you could be asked any time you are networking or in a professional conversation or interview.
- ▹ After each question, there are two answers. Determine which is the better answer and why.
- ▹ Also identify the skills that appear in each question and write those in the space provided.

Question A: What skills did you develop at your job before law school? (sales for a tech company)

Take #1

When I worked in sales, I focused on listening closely to what a client wanted and then ensuring that the product met those needs. I had this one client who was so polite and never said anything bad, but I could tell that she and her team were not thrilled about our product. I started asking a lot of questions to better understand her team's needs. It turned out that there was one really important feature they weren't utilizing in our product. Once we realized this and taught her team how to use that feature, they were much happier. I enjoyed the problem-solving aspects of the job, especially when working with clients. I am naturally a little shy, but I got over that quickly because I talked to people and did group presentations and cold calls all day.

3. Adapted from The George Washington University Law School Inns of Court Program, 2018 (Co-Directors: Todd Peterson and Susan Fine; Dean of Students: Elizabeth Ewert).

Name the skills demonstrated in this response (if any):

Take #2

I had to learn all about the specific technology we were selling. We had these playbooks that had a ton of frequently asked questions, and I had to memorize the answers to common questions corporate clients might have. I had this one client who always asked me a lot of questions, and I remember thinking, I'm so glad I memorized all these answers because I think I recited that entire playbook to that client. I learned how to talk my way through a lot of situations, especially during group presentations. And I learned to talk fast because I usually only had about one to two minutes to talk with potential new clients when I would cold-call people I met at the vendor booth at conferences.

Name the skills demonstrated in this response (if any):

Circle which response is better:

TAKE #1	TAKE #2

Why is that response better?

____

____

____

Question B: Based on Take #1 and Take #2 in this section, write what you think the question being asked is:

____

____

____

Take #1

I want to get started working in the legal field because I know I'm not going to do sales anymore. I am a hard worker and there's no job too small for me. I'm eager to learn and get training, and I believe you provide a lot of training and support for new hires. There is a good variety in the work here, and I heard you can do pro bono work, which I like. The culture also seems like a really good fit for my personality.

Name the skills demonstrated in this response (if any):

Take #2

I think I'll be able to handle a large amount of responsibility quickly, and I enjoy being part of a team, which I know is a quality you said you are looking for. At my sales job, when our team manager unexpectedly got sick with the flu, they needed someone to step in ASAP to finish drafting a sales proposal to a possible client. Although I had not written a sales proposal before, I always read them when we won a new account, and so I offered to step in and help. The team and other managers were grateful. They all helped me write it, and we won the account! We worked really well together in quickly finishing the draft, and I got to know other sales managers I likely never would have worked with otherwise.

Name the skills demonstrated in this response (if any):

Circle which response is better:

TAKE #1	TAKE #2

Why is that response better?

____

____

____

Question C: What did you think about your first year in law school?

Take #1

It was hard and stressful. I've never read so much in my life! It wasn't the amount of reading but rather reading case law that was difficult. I'm hardworking and take to most tasks, and my first year was no different. I'm used to working hard, and that's what I did.

Name the skills demonstrated in this response (if any):

Take #2

It was definitely challenging, but once I found my rhythm, it got a lot better. In my first month, I was outlining by writing in my books, but I soon realized I retained the information better if I read the case and tried to write out the holding in my outline. I'd go to office hours if I still didn't understand something, and I'd edit my outline again after class. In the end, finding a system that worked for me ended up helping me save time and understand the information better.

Name the skills demonstrated in this response (if any):

Circle which response is better:

TAKE #1	TAKE #2

Why is that response better?

____

____

____

4. Activity: Your Turn: Oral Communication and Applying Active Listening Skills[4]

As you know, oral communication and active listening are critical skills identified in Chapter 1. This exercise will focus on both. It will also require you to "think on your feet" by imposing time limits on your preparation and your presentation.

---

4. *See* R. Lisle Baker, *Designing a Positive Psychology Course for Lawyers*, 51 Suffolk U. L. Rev. 207, 247 (2018) (using feedback forms to practice focused attention as students listen to in-class presentations), https://ssrn.com/abstract=3271713. Thiadora Pina is indebted to R. Lisle Baker for providing this paper.

Instructions: Part A

There are two parts to this activity. The first part asks you to develop your "talking points" and is useful for:

- ▹ networking and business development
- ▹ interviews and informational interviews
- ▹ events
- ▹ client service and building relationships

For this part of the activity you will:

1	Review the STAR method example below.
2	Choose one of your top skills, interests, or values and draft an example that illustrates the qualities you bring to an employer by using the STAR method format. This will be your example for this exercise.
3	Present your example to the class. **Note:** Although you may initially resist the idea of presenting to the class, this exercise is what you will be asked to do as a legal intern and lawyer. When you first begin working in the legal profession, your knowledge and skills are limited compared to the more senior lawyers with whom you will work. Regardless of your experience, you will constantly have to present your ideas, thoughts, and action plans. Even in a work environment, this is not always comfortable or easy!
4	Your presentation *must* follow the following format (no exceptions): • Three-minute presentation time (*Anecdote to Illustrate* column in the next table) • Two minutes to explain the specific competencies identified in your story (*Value to Employer* column) Note that these are strict time limits!

Part A: Oral Communication

Don't worry if your examples do not arise in a legal context. They can arise from any part of your life. You will add to your bank of legal examples as you gain legal experience.

Examples that are woven into concise and coherent anecdotes are the best way to demonstrate you have the relevant skills that employers and clients need and want. Anecdotes are entertaining and memorable, and you want to be both engaging and remembered. Your anecdotes should be brief, with a beginning, middle, and end. The STAR formula is a helpful organizing tool:

- **Situation or Task**: Describe the situation that you were in or the task that you needed to accomplish. You must describe a specific event or situation, not a generalized description of what you have done in the past. Be sure to give enough detail to set the scene. This situation can be from a previous job, volunteer experience, or any relevant event.
- **Action** you took: Describe the action you took and be sure to keep the focus on you. Even if you are discussing a group project or effort, describe what *you* did—not the efforts of the team. Describe exactly what you actually did (not what you might do in a future instance).
- **Results** you achieved: What was the outcome? How did the event end? What did you accomplish? What did you learn? The results should identify your value-add for an employer.

STAR Example

Skill	How Acquired?	Anecdote to Illustrate	Value to Employer
Project Management	Created speaker series for political science department	S/T: The department asked me to identify, contact, and schedule four high-profile speakers with different viewpoints on the primary process. A: From discussions in class, I already knew who we wanted to invite, but I didn't know who would be interested and available. So I had to generate a list of alternatives, making sure to maintain the balance in perspectives that we were seeking. It was a bit tricky to map out the schedule, but I gave each potential speaker a choice of dates and could offer an honorarium so long as I didn't exceed the total budget allotted. When the speakers were in place, I arranged the venues and publicized each event to increase attendance. R: All the planning really paid off. By breaking down the project into subtasks and having contingency plans, I was able to meet all the deadlines, and the series came together smoothly and went very well.	* **Project management skills:** - Using time efficiently - Managing a budget - Completing projects by deadline - Working well under pressure and with others Other: * **Communication skills**

Your Turn: STAR Presentations

Skill	How Acquired?	Value to Employer

Anecdote to Illustrate:

____

____

____

____

____

____

____

____

____

Applying Active Listening Skills

Instructions: Part B

Here you will demonstrate a different critical skill, namely "listen attentively and respectfully, including habit of actively seeking feedback." For this part of the activity you will:

Part B: Listen Attentively

1	Practice the skill of active listening as your peers present their value propositions, and then offer positive/helpful feedback.
2	You will partner with a colleague and present to each other. You will offer feedback on their presentation on the provided one-page form, summarizing the main points (as you understood them) and offering constructive suggestions. See the Coaching Your Colleague—Presentation Feedback Form below. **Note:** These forms are representative of what you will be asked to do as lawyers and professionals. We are asked to provide feedback all the time! When you have an internship/externship, for example, your supervising attorney or judge often will ask you, "What do you think?" Thus, this feedback form gives you a chance to practice a skill you soon will use all the time.

3	**Note:** You may find it easier to switch workbooks with your colleague so that you may write your feedback directly into their workbook. You are welcome to decide how this is accomplished. Notwithstanding, each of you must present and each of you must complete a Feedback Form that you give to your colleague.

Coaching Your Colleague—Presentation Feedback Form[5]

As your peers present their value propositions, this is an opportunity for you to practice your active listening skills by applying your focused attention to their presentations. You will complete this form, noting what you heard and offering feedback to each peer on their presentation.

Speaker Name	Your Name as Coach

Active listening: As I understood you, the principal idea(s) you offered are . . .

---

5. R. Lisle Baker, *Integrating Positive Psychology into Legal Education*, 48 SOUTHWEST. L. REV. 295 (2019) (summarizing national conferences on this topic held at Suffolk University Law School in 2017 and 2018 by organizing the participant presentations thematically around some of the important features of legal education—critical thinking, competition, independence, diligence, and professional values—and how to complement those features in ways that enhance the well-being and success of students, as well as the legal educators who teach them; also supplemented by links to the written materials prepared by the participants in the conferences so that readers of the article can dive deeper into a specific presentation and find additional resources).

Offering Feedback: Have you considered the following additional ideas to further build on your good start on this exercise?

6

Setting Goals and Problem Solving

Moving from Student to Lawyer

LEARNING OUTCOMES

- Design activities to help develop your professional identity while in law school, while at your legal internship/externship, and while practicing law.
- Define and select SMART goals to continue moving along the professional development and self-directedness continuum.
- Define and use problem-solving techniques to choose appropriate professional paths forward.

Reflection: Part A

Learning Objectives Self-Assessment

- To complete the following self-assessment exercise, read through the table below. The table lists the learning objectives from the previous chapter.
- If you can satisfy the objective, place a check mark in the box.
- If you do not understand the objective or if you have more questions about the objective, place a question mark in the box.

Note: You need solid evidence to support your choices. Here, your solid evidence is the ability to accomplish the stated learning objective.

AT THIS POINT, YOU SHOULD BE ABLE TO:	
	Describe the process, benefits, and link between networking and business development.
	Analyze and measure your progress/benchmarks in developing a networking plan.
	Define the STAR method and develop, choose, and communicate appropriate STAR method examples.
	Explain and apply active listening skills to oral communication.

Reflection: Part B

Self-Directedness and Using Reflective Practice: Networking and Business Development

This is the *Reflective Practice* rubric introduced in Chapter 3. This time, however, you are reflecting on your networking efforts and plans identified in Chapter 5. Here you will continue to demonstrate solid professional development by purposely engaging in and tracking your reflective practice for Chapter 5.

For *Steps 3 & 4* in the following table, think about these two things: (1) the networking efforts and plans you identified in your Chapter 5 Pre-Class Work and (2) the anecdotes you relied upon in your Chapter 5 Pre-Class Work.

Also, remember that you must *always* rely on objective evidence to support your level of development. In other words, to support your chosen level, you need to have *solid evidence* that legal employers would value. If you do not have that solid evidence, you must then *describe your plan for obtaining that evidence* (which demonstrates problem solving).

Exercise: Using Reflective Practice: Networking and Business Development

Refer back to Chapter 3 for complete instructions on how to complete this assignment. Abbreviated instructions are provided below.

Steps **1** & **2**	**Reflect** Using the *Reflective Practice* rubric from Chapter 3, answer the question "What level am I currently at?" & **Explain** • **What?** The "what" is always the subject of the reflective practice for the week. For this assignment, you will reflect on your top values from Chapter 4. • **So what?** What is the anecdote you will use to answer the preceding question, including describing the lesson(s) learned? • **Now what?** What adjustments will you make next time? How can you put this part of your answer into context for legal employers and attorneys? Using "critical skill language" will help here.

<table>
<tr><td rowspan="4">Steps 3 & 4</td><td>Novice Learner</td><td rowspan="4">Appraise & Assess
Circle your current level of development and then provide solid evidence for your selection.</td></tr>
<tr><td>Intermediate Learner</td></tr>
<tr><td>Competent Learner</td></tr>
<tr><td>Exceptional Learner</td></tr>
</table>

Pre-Class Work

The Venn diagram introduced in Chapter 4—after you identified your skills, values, and interests—helped you visualize concrete ways that law school can help you on your professional identity path as you move from student to lawyer.

As noted in Chapter 4, "you must take full advantage of the many ways law school can help you build your professional identity." The following exercises will help you do exactly that.

You should effectively use your remaining semesters in law school, as well as school summer and winter breaks, to build your professional identity and achieve your goals. Below you will focus on how to draft and measure goals, the resources available to help you achieve those goals, and next steps in communicating your goals to lawyers and legal employers.

1. Self-Directedness and SMART Goals

As you know, Professional Development and Self-Directedness is a critical skill, and the full rubric to measure your progress in developing and demonstrating this skill was introduced in Chapter 2. You will revisit this rubric now, moving to the next sub-competency: *Articulates Goals and Follows a Plan.*

To effectively use your remaining time in law school, you must have a plan. For this exercise, you will focus on the Articulates Goals and Follows a Plan sub-competency within the Self-Directedness skill rubric. You will develop a plan and draft SMART goals for your remaining time in law school.

Self-Directedness Competency: Articulates Goals and Follows a Plan

Rarely creates and implements a written professional development plan reflecting goals that are specific, measurable, achievable, relevant, and time-bound.	**Sometimes** creates and implements a written professional development plan reflecting goals that are specific, measurable, achievable, relevant, and time-bound.	**Often** creates and implements a written professional development plan reflecting goals that are specific, measurable, achievable, relevant, and time-bound.	**Consistently** creates and implements a written professional development plan reflecting goals that are specific, measurable, achievable, relevant, and time-bound.

Part of building your professional identity is knowing or having a plan for where you are going and how you are going to get there. Of course, it is always okay to adjust, change, or abandon plans altogether, especially at this stage of your legal career.

I have been a law professor for many years, and I have witnessed countless students enter their first year of law school as soon-to-be "public defenders," "corporate" lawyers, or "in-house" lawyers, only to graduate and practice an entirely different area of law.

You cannot be pigeonholed as a first-year or second-year law student. But, redefining your legal career does become more difficult the longer you practice a specific area of law. For example, if you are a five-year practicing family law lawyer who wakes up one day and decides to practice real estate conveyancing, that leap is not impossible, but it will be a substantial and very difficult leap! Either way, both the first-year law student and the five-year practicing family law lawyer in the example above, must create a professional development plan.

Thus, creating a plan for your remaining time in law school is important—refining, changing, adding items to, and perhaps taking away items from that plan is also important. You must move along the above rubric to demonstrate solid evidence of your self-directedness. If you rarely create and implement a professional development plan, you must start. If you do this consistently, then congratulations, and with this assignment you will keep up that very good work!

2. Create a Plan[1]

Instructions:

- Begin by answering the questions below. These questions are designed to get you to think strategically about structuring your remaining time in law school. Law school will go by quickly! You must plan your remaining semesters well.
- Consider which classes and opportunities you may want to take, and think broadly. Remember the Venn diagram from Chapter 4 showing that you have many options at your disposal, including informational interviews, courses, clinics, externships, events, panels, student organizations, bar associations, etc.

1. Adapted from *The Roadmap Template: Planning My Remaining Time in Law School* authored by Neil W. Hamilton, Carl J. L. Numrich, Bryan M. Wachter and Colin Seaborg.

1. List three of your strongest skills from the critical skills list in Chapter 1.

1	
2	
3	

2. What will you do to further develop these skills? What experiences, both inside and outside of law school, will help you further develop these skills, thus providing the solid evidence you need to both continue moving from student to lawyer and to communicate to legal employers? Write out a plan for each of the skills listed above.

1	
2	
3	

3. What courses will you take to highlight the skills you listed above, and when are those courses offered? Name the courses specifically. You may also include additional skills from Class 1.

1	**Course:** **Will strengthen my skills by:**
2	**Course:** **Will strengthen my skills by:**
3	**Course:** **Will strengthen my skills by:**

4. What other non-curricular choices will you make to highlight the critical skills from Chapter 1, for example, student organization memberships, accomplishments, externships/internships, pro bono service, general community activities, or bar activities? Be specific.

• Skill or interest highlighted: • Non-curricular choice:
• Skill or interest highlighted: • Non-curricular choice:

5. Your Chapter 5 Networking Exercise is also part of planning your remaining time in law school.
   - How will your networking plan help you gain experiences that will be useful for further developing your professional identity?
   - Who will your plan put you in contact with and why? Focus especially on senior people who will mentor and coach you.

6. What is your biggest fear, roadblock, or obstacle(s) that may hold you back from any of the steps outlined above?

3. Developing and Choosing SMART Goals

Goal setting is a component of professional development. The *Self-Directedness* rubric shown above tells us that part of that skill is to "create and implement a written professional development plan reflecting goals that are specific, measurable, achievable, relevant, and time-bound."

And research also "suggests that envisioning a successful future, along with the potential obstacles and how they might be overcome" can aid successful goal setting.[1]

1. *See* R. Lisle Baker, *Designing a Positive Psychology Course for Lawyers*, 51 SUFFOLK U. L. REV. 207, 251 (2018) (goal setting producing positive outcomes through visualizing success, obstacles to success, and how they can be overcome), https://ssrn.com/abstract=3271713. Thiadora Pina is indebted to R. Lisle Baker for providing this paper.

So, there is more to goal setting than simply stating the goal; after all, there is a difference between a goal (development) and a wish (hope).

When the *Self-Directedness* rubric states that goals must be specific, measurable, achievable, relevant, and time-bound (SMART), here is how SMART goals are further defined.

Sub-Competencies of Ownership/Self-Directedness Rubric

Sub-Competencies of Ownership/ Self-Directedness	Novice Student (Level 1)	Advanced Beginner (Level 2)	Intermediate (Level 3)	Student at Graduation (Level 4)	Junior Attorney (Level 5)
Meets learning needs by defining SMART goals: **Specific—** clear goal, including what (name the competency), why, and how **Measurable—** including a clear method for evaluation of progress **Achievable—** including obstacles and realistic solutions **Relevant—** including connection to core values **Time-bound—** including a clear timeline of steps	**Needs significant assistance** to identify and articulate a SMART goal. Rarely articulates goals to meet learning needs that meet all criteria for all five SMART goals.	**Can describe** what SMART goals are and can articulate a goal that meets all five elements with **some coaching.** Occasionally articulates goals to meet learning needs that meet all criteria for all five SMART goals.	**Can apply** the SMART goals framework and articulates goals that meet all five elements. Frequently articulates goals to meet learning needs that meet all criteria for all five SMART goals.	**Can explain** the reasons for setting SMART goals and is able to do so in a variety of situations. **Almost always articulates goals** to meet learning needs that meet all criteria for all five SMART goals.	**Can teach** others how to apply the SMART goals framework to goal setting. **Always articulates goals to meet learning needs** that meet all criteria for all five SMART goals.

Instructions: SMART Goals Assignment

- Identify a job that is currently posted on the internet. This may be a "dream job" you hope to obtain far in the future or a job you would like to apply for after graduation—you decide. The goal is to find a legal position, currently posted, which interests you and that you want to do. This job should equate to "meaningful employment" for you.
- Do not chose a legal position that you will hold as a law student. Choose a legal position that starts *after* graduation, at the earliest.
- Now, armed with that job description and using the SMART Goals chart above, start with Step 1 below and draft three SMART goals.
- These SMART goals will help you move closer to obtaining and demonstrating the competencies you must acquire to successfully apply for and obtain the job you chose. In other words, your goal is to articulate the experiences you will need to develop in order to demonstrate the critical skills and competencies your future job requires.

Sub-Competencies of Ownership / Self-Directedness Rubric

Step 1	Write out three SMART goals that will move you closer to acquiring the competencies you need to apply for your selected job. For the T (Time-bound), use the following timeframes: • Winter/Summer break • During the next year • Before graduation	
SMART Goal #1	**SMART Goal #2**	**SMART Goal #3**
S:	S:	S:
M:	M:	M:
A:	A:	A:

R:	R:	R:
T: Winter/Summer break	T: During the next year	T: Before graduation

Any additional considerations?

Step **2**	**Assessment of Student's Ownership of Continuous Professional Development (Self-Directedness): Meets Learning Needs by Defining SMART Goals** Review the *Self-Directedness Competency and Articulates Goals and Follows a Plan* rubric above. Because you are now comfortable with using rubrics to assess your level of development regarding your professional identity and critical lawyering skills, you will do so here in relation to the SMART goals you just drafted. As you know, if you do not have an answer for what you will affirmatively do, you *must* articulate your plan for finding the answer (diagnose learning needs).
Step **3**	Review the rubric and circle your level of development in the following chart, relying on your written SMART goals as objective evidence of your choice.
Step **4**	Articulate the reasons for the selection you made regarding your level of development.

	Appraise & Assess
Novice Student	**Appraise & Assess** Circle your current level of development. Provide solid evidence for your selection.
Advanced Beginner	
Intermediate	
Student at Graduation	
Junior Attorney	

4. Prepare SMART Goals Presentation

Instructions:

- Select one goal which you will present in class and then create a PowerPoint (or Google Slides) presentation of that one goal. Your PowerPoint slide(s) will follow Step 1 above and also meet these requirements:
  - The first slide will contain the job description you selected.
  - The remaining slides will list and clearly articulate each S-M-A-R-T Goal component.
  - You must be prepared and ready to present when called. Your goal must be SMART and clearly meet the parameters of each SMART component.

Pre-Class Work Complete

In-Class Activity

1. Class Discussion: Review of Class 5

- Measuring Learning Objectives (Self-Assessment): Questions and Comments
- Ownership of Continuous Professional Development: Using Reflective Practice in Networking, Business Development, and Communicating Your Value Proposition

2. Class Discussion: Identify Activities Related to Your Professional Identity with Your Remaining Time in Law School

- Identify the links between Chapters 4, 5, and 6

3. In-Class Presentations: SMART Goals: Planning, Timeframes, and Professional Development

SMART Goals PowerPoint Presentations

- Each student will present one SMART goal using PowerPoint (or Google Slides).

4. Coaching Your Colleagues: Presentation Feedback Forms

- Demonstrate active listening skills while offering solid and constructive feedback to your peers. You will complete a feedback form for each presentation.

7

Developing Your Professional Development Plan

LEARNING OUTCOMES

- Take ownership of your professional identity by demonstrating movement along the Assessment of Student's Ownership of Continuous Professional Development (Self-Directedness).
- Choosing meaningful opportunities that allow you to match your skills, interests, and values to your professional identity as you serve legal employers, clients, and the legal profession.

Reflection: Part A

Learning Objectives Self-Assessment

- To complete the following self-assessment exercise, read through the table below. The table lists the learning objectives from the previous chapter.
- If you can satisfy the objective, place a check mark in the box.
- If you do not understand the objective or if you have more questions about the objective, place a question mark in the box.

Note: You need solid evidence to support your choices. Here, your solid evidence is the ability to accomplish the stated learning objective.

AT THIS POINT, YOU SHOULD BE ABLE TO:	
	Describe the process, benefits, and link between networking and business development.
	Analyze and measure your progress/benchmarks in developing a networking plan.
	Define the STAR method and develop, choose, and communicate appropriate STAR method examples.
	Explain and apply active listening skills to oral communication.

Reflection: Part B

Self-Directedness and Using Reflective Practice: Networking and Business Development

This is the *Reflective Practice* rubric introduced in Chapter 3. This time, however, you are reflecting on your SMART goals and plans identified in Chapter 6. Here you will continue to demonstrate solid professional development by purposely engaging in and tracking your reflective practice for Chapter 6.

For *Steps 3 & 4* in the following table, think about these two things: (1) the SMART goals and plans you identified in your Chapter 6 Pre-Class Work and (2) the anecdotes you relied upon in your Chapter 6 Pre-Class Work.

Also, remember that you must *always* rely on objective evidence to support your level of development. In other words, you need to have *solid evidence* that legal employers would value to support your chosen level. If you do not have that solid evidence, you must then *describe your plan for obtaining that evidence* (which demonstrates problem solving).

Exercise: Using Reflective Practice: SMART Goals and Problem Solving

Refer back to Chapter 3 for complete instructions on how to complete this assignment. Abbreviated instructions are provided below.

<table>
<tr><td>Steps
1
&
2</td><td>Reflect
Using the Reflective Practice rubric from Chapter 3, answer the question "What level am I currently at?"
&
Explain
• What? The "what" is always the subject of the reflective practice for the week. For this assignment, you will reflect on your top values from Chapter 6.
• So what? What is the anecdote you will use to answer the preceding question, including describing the lesson(s) learned?
• Now what? What adjustments will you make next time? How can you put this part of your answer into context for legal employers and attorneys? Using "critical skill language" will help here.</td></tr>
</table>

<table>
<tr><td rowspan="4">Steps
3
&
4</td><td>Novice Learner</td><td rowspan="4">Appraise & Assess
Circle your current level of development and then provide solid evidence for your selection.</td></tr>
<tr><td>Intermediate Learner</td></tr>
<tr><td>Competent Learner</td></tr>
<tr><td>Exceptional Learner</td></tr>
</table>

Pre-Class Work

> *"By now, it should be absolutely clear that you must... take ownership over your continuous development of the competencies required to meet employers' and clients' needs."*[1]

Welcome to Class 7 and your final assignment! Your activities this week will help you demonstrate your development to date, and ask you to prepare and to communicate your plan moving forward.

1. Draft Your Elevator Pitch after Completing the CLS Workbook

Instructions:

- Based on what you have learned and how your professional identity has grown, revisit and update the elevator pitch that you drafted in your Chapter 1 Pre-Class Work.
- For this assignment you are answering the following question: what is my elevator pitch after completing this course?
- Remember, your elevator pitch is a living thing. It will continue to change over the course of your career as you achieve and upgrade your goals and when you need to highlight different strengths, values, skills, accomplishments, and goals for different audiences.

Things to consider including in your new Elevator Pitch:

- Your goals
- Classes you plan to take
- Externships/internships you will complete or about which you want to find more information
- Your connections and mentors
- People with whom you plan to meet and plans you have to address regarding your ongoing learning needs.

1. *See* Neil W. Hamilton, Roadmap: THE LAW STUDENT'S GUIDE TO MEANINGFUL EMPLOYMENT 17 (2023).

Elevator Pitch after Completing CLS

____

____

____

____

____

2. Compare and Contrast Value Propositions: Self-Assessment from Chapter 1 to Chapter 7

Instructions:

- ▹ After drafting your elevator pitch for Chapter 7, compare and contrast it to your elevator pitch from Chapter 1. Assess all major changes and additions, and then describe those by using the template that follows.

Box 1: Be specific in your description. Explain why and how your value proposition changed.

Box 2: Choose from the learning objectives (found at the beginning of each chapter) and select two of the objectives that support the changes you identified in Box 1. In other words, two class learning objectives will be the solid evidence that you rely upon in assessing the changes you identified between your Chapter 1 and Chapter 7 Elevator Pitches.

Box 3: Demonstrate your professional identity development with solid evidence by tracking your movement along any of the rubrics used in this CLS Workbook. Choose two new learning objectives (different from the ones you chose for Box 2), and indicate a specific way you moved or increased your development level for any of the following rubrics or self-assessments:

- ▹ *The Assessment of Student's Ownership of Continuous Professional Development (Self-Directedness)* rubric (Chapter 1)
- ▹ *The Growth Mindset* rubric (Chapter 4)
- ▹ *Law Student's Networking Skills Development* rubric (Chapter 5)
- ▹ The *SMART Goals* rubric (Chapter 6)

If you can't specifically identify a level increase along at least one of these rubrics, then you must diagnose your learning needs and state your plan for accomplishing that move. In other words, what will you do—what specific action plan will you implement—to move to the next level in at least one of the rubrics?

Box 4: Describe your plan to move to the next level in any one of the above rubrics. Specifically identify the rubric you are using and be sure to provide *solid evidence* in describing the action steps you will take to accomplish the move.

Box **1**	**Why and how your Elevator Pitch changed from Class 1 to Class 7:**
Box **2**	**Your Class 7 Elevator Pitch demonstrates the following class learning objectives:** • Learning objective 1: __________ __________ • From class: __________ • How demonstrated: __________ __________ __________ __________ __________ __________ • Learning objective 2: __________ __________ • From class: __________ • How demonstrated: __________ __________ __________ __________ __________ __________

Box 3	**One *specific* way you moved or increased your development level this semester:** • Name of rubric: ____________________ ____________________ • From class: ____________________ • How demonstrated: ____________________ ____________________ ____________________ ____________________ ____________________ ____________________ ____________________ ____________________ ____________________
Box 4	**My plan to move to the next level in one of the rubrics is:** • Name of rubric: ____________________ ____________________ • From class: ____________________ • How demonstrated: ____________________ ____________________ ____________________ ____________________ ____________________ ____________________ ____________________ ____________________ ____________________

3. Discuss and Present Elevator Pitch Changes

Instructions:

- ▹ Select one example from Box 1, 2, 3, or 4.
- ▹ Be ready to present that example during the Class 7 In-Class Activity. Prepare and practice your presentation before class and be organized and succinct.
- ▹ Your presentation may include PowerPoint slides, but this is not required. Your presentation must be organized and clear.

4. Build Course Learning into a Future Action: Design Your Professional Development Plan (PDP)

For this class, you will demonstrate your understanding and development of course learning objectives and connect your skills, interests, and values to your professional identity by drafting your PDP.

Draft Your Professional Development Plan

Instructions:

- ▹ There are three parts to this assignment:
  1. the PDP template,
  2. the PDP reflection essay, and
  3. preparing for in-class discussion.

1

PDP Template
Using your job description from Class 6, please complete the following template.

With your SMART goals (from Class 6) in mind, you will draft your PDP essay. However, you will complete the PDP template first. In this section, as you complete the template and describe how you will get from where you are today to where you want to be (your job description), be thoughtful, concise, and organized. Your professor must be able to clearly follow your PDP template entries.

Fill out the *entire* template. Do not skip any steps. Your PDP *must* include:

- Your strongest competencies and how they relate to your job description
- Your learning needs (the "Now what?" parts of the reflections you completed for Pre-Class Work, or areas you must develop to obtain the job you have selected)

	• Your values and how they relate to this job • Any additional areas of law and employers in which you have an interest • Roles, opportunities, and experiences you may have or need before you are ready to begin your (dream) job
2	**PDP Reflection Essay** After completing the PDP template, you will summarize your PDP template and draft a short PDP reflection essay. Your essay will have three sections and follow the (now familiar!) reflection prompt: • **What?** This is the skills and values section of your PDP template: the unique talents and skills you possess that will also benefit your future legal employer and clients. • **So what?** *(consider multiple perspectives, including your own, and contemplate lessons learned)* This is the learning needs section of your PDP template: the feedback you have sought and received, and the knowledge you have gained in law school. It also asks "What more do you need to do?" • **Now what?** *(identify how to apply lessons learned to improve in the future)* This is the "additional areas and roles" section of the PDP template. How will you proceed? What next steps will you take? What's your action plan to move forward toward integrating your professional identity (skills, values, interests) with finding meaningful employment that benefits you and the legal employer?
3	Be prepared to discuss the process of creating your PDP during the in-class discussion. What did you include and why? What surprised you about your PDP, and how do you anticipate that it will continue to evolve?

Professional Development Plan (PDP)

	My Strongest Skills	How My Strongest Skills Relate to the Job Description
1		
2		

	My Values	How My Values Relate to the Job Description
1		
2		

Additional Areas of Law and Employers in Which I Have an Interest
1.
2.
3.

	Additional Roles, Opportunities, or Experiences Needed for Job Description	What Additional Skills Do I Need, and How Will I Address My Learning Needs to Acquire Them?
EXAMPLE	If your job description has a title attached to it, such as General Counsel or Director, generally you will need to be a senior-level associate or an assistant director first. This section asks you to identify which experiences you will need first to reach the level your job description requires.	
1		
2		
3		

5. Submit Your PDP Reflection Essay

Instructions:

Upload your PDP Reflection Essay directly, by either emailing your professor or uploading your assignment to your class learning management system. Be sure to follow the instructions above.

Pre-Class Work Complete

In-Class Activity

1. Class Presentation: Professional Development Plans (PDPs)

- Discuss the results of creating your PDP.
- Demonstrate your understanding of the course learning objectives; demonstrate your own professional development and growth by connecting your skills, interests, and values to your professional identity.
- Your presentation may include PowerPoint slides, but this is not required. Your presentation must be organized and clear.

2. Class Presentation: Elevator Pitch Changes

- Demonstrate your growth and progress along the professional development continuum and present changes from your Chapter 1 to Chapter 7 Elevator Pitch.

3. Demonstrate Active Listening Skills by Completing Feedback Forms

- **Feedback Forms:** Each student will complete a feedback form and provide constructive feedback to each of their colleagues.

Final Reflection

- To complete the following self-assessment exercise, read through the table below. The table lists the learning objectives from the previous chapter.
- If you can satisfy the objective, place a check mark in the box.
- If you do not understand the objective or if you have more questions about the objective, place a question mark in the box.

Note: You need solid evidence to support your choices. Here, your solid evidence is the ability to accomplish the stated learning objective.

After completing this class, you should be able to:	
	Take ownership of your professional identity by demonstrating movement along the Assessment of Student's Ownership of Continuous Professional Development (Self-Directedness).
	Choosing meaningful opportunities that allow you to match your skills, interests, and values to your professional identity as you serve legal employers, clients, and the legal profession.

Good luck!

Appendix I

Top Critical Skills

Negotiation skills	Stress/crisis management	Leadership
Delegation, supervision, mentoring	Initiative/drive/strong work ethic	Provide high quality legal advice
Problem solving / good judgment, including appropriately engaging supervisor	Pro bono, community, bar association involvement	Listen attentively and respectfully, including habit of actively seeking feedback
Integrity/honesty/trustworthiness, including building relationships (networking)	Analytical skills/law knowledge, including legal research	Commitment to firm/department and its goals and values
Ability to work independently	Interview clients and witnesses	Effective communication skills—oral and written
High quality work product, managing own work and multiple tasks (project management)	Initiates and maintains strong team and work relationships	Dedication and understanding of clients and client service, including promptly responding to all inquiries and requests

Appendix II

Remember, your resume is a marketing tool to highlight your relevant competencies and critical skills for your next employer. Thus, the skills important to that employer must be demonstrated in the descriptions of your experiences and your critical skills.

This Resume Toolkit includes a checklist to assist in your overall updates and a list of action verbs to assist in your description updates. It is a good idea to have a "master resume" and then tailor specific resumes to specific employers or types of employers.

Resume Checklist

Overall Formatting

- Does your information fill the page and not look crowded?
- Have you selected an easy-to-read font: e.g., Times New Roman, Arial, Calibri, 11–12pt?
- Have you structured the page in an easy to read way, e.g., bullet points or paragraphs (not both)?
- Has your formatting remained consistent across all positions? (For example, if you've bolded job titles, are *all* job titles bolded?)
- Are your margins even?
- Are all items aligned? E.g., if you've right-aligned dates, are they all lining up with one another?
- Have you checked there are no typos or errors?
- Have you edited it for brevity? (Try to keep your resume to about one page if possible.)
- Have you converted your resume to a format that allows all recipients to read it as intended? (PDF format is recommended unless specifically stated otherwise in application instructions.)

Contact Information / Letterhead

- Have you included your contact information: name, address, email address, and phone number?
- Is your email address professional? (e.g. dporter@scu.edu vs. surfdude@gmail.com)
- If you are looking for opportunities in a different geographic location, have you indicated an address for that other geographic location, and/or explained your interest in moving to a different geographical location in your cover letter?

Education Section

- Have you included relevant information about your education such as school, degree, GPA (maybe), activities and awards? (Note: you are obtaining a Juris Doctor or Doctor of Jurisprudence degree, not a Juris Doctorate)
- Have you checked for consistency in how you describe your education? (e.g., Juris Doctor and Bachelor of Arts or J.D. and B.A.)

Experience Section & Other Relevant Sections

- Have you included your employer name, your title, location, month and date you were at each job?
- Have you customized your resume for the specific job you're applying to? (Highlight work experience and skills that are relevant to the position—don't just write down everything you've ever done professionally.)
- Have you added additional skills such as languages and software relevant to the industry, and interests such as anything that points to your personality or interests outside of work?
- Have you included action verbs and keywords in your resume? (see list next page)

Action Verbs Used To Describe Skills Utilized By Lawyers

accomplished	caused	described	granted	observed	recruited
achieved	chaired	designed	grouped	obtained	reorganized
acquired	classified	determined	guided	opened	replied
adapted	collaborated	developed	headed	ordered	represented
added	collected	devised	highlighted	organized	required
adjusted	combined	diagnosed	identified	originated	researched
administered	communicated	directed	implemented	oversaw	resolved
advised	compared	discovered	improved	participated	responded
allocated	compiled	dispensed	incorporated	perceived	restored
analyzed	completed	distributed	increased	performed	reviewed
answered	conceived	documented	indexed	persuaded	revised
anticipated	conceptualized	drafted	influenced	planned	scheduled
appeared	concluded	earned	initiated	prepared	searched
applied	conducted	edited	inspected	prescribed	selected
appointed	conserved	effected	installed	presented	settled
appraised	considered	enlarged	instituted	prevailed	solved
approved	consolidated	established	instructed	processed	specialized
argued	constructed	estimated	integrated	procured	specified
arranged	consulted	evaluated	interpreted	produced	started
articulated	contracted	examined	interrogated	programmed	strategized
assembled	controlled	executed	interviewed	prohibited	strengthened
assessed	converted	expanded	introduced	projected	studied
assigned	convinced	expedited	invented	promoted	submitted
assumed	coordinated	experienced	investigated	proofed	suggested
attained	corrected	explored	involved	proposed	summarized
attended	corresponded	expressed	joined	prosecuted	supervised
audited	counseled	extended	lectured	proved	surveyed
authored	created	facilitated	led	provided	targeted
authorized	critiqued	financed	lobbied	published	taught
awarded	dealt	focused	maintained	purchased	tested
began	debated	forecast	managed	pursued	trained
bolstered	decided	formed	mediated	questioned	translated
briefed	deduced	formulated	moderated	qualified	traveled
budgeted	defended	fostered	modified	quantified	tutored
built	defined	founded	monitored	ranked	unified
calculated	delegated	gained	motivated	rated	updated
catalogued	delivered	gathered	navigated	recommended	verified
caught	demonstrated	generated	negotiated	recorded	won

Index

V

W